CHAMPIONS

CHAMPIONS

The Making of Olympic Swimmers

Daniel F. Chambliss

William Morrow and Company, Inc. New York

Library of Congress Cataloging-in-Publication Data

Chambliss, Daniel F.
    Champions : the making of Olympic swimmers.

    1. Swimming—United States. 2. Olympics.
I. Title.
GV838.4.U6C48   1988   797.2'1   87-31497
ISBN 0-688-07618-1

Printed in the United States of America

First Edition

1 2 3 4 5 6 7 8 9 10

BOOK DESIGN BY PANDORA SPELIOS

This book is dedicated to
my old and irreplaceable friend Joe Harris.

Contents

It is abhorrent to my soul to talk inhumanly about greatness, to let it loom darkly at a distance in an indefinite form, to make out that it is great without making the human character of it evident— wherewith it ceases to be great.

—Søren Kierkegaard

PROLOGUE

A Day Like Any Other

IT'S FIVE-FIFTEEN ON A JANUARY MORNING IN SOUTHERN California. The temperature in the near-desert air is in the high forties; above the surrounding mountains the sky is just beginning to lighten. In the very center of the valley, over a huge rectangular swimming pool—more than fifty yards long and exactly twenty-five yards wide—clouds of fog float, hanging over water that is constantly heated to eighty degrees. The murmur of young voices is heard. The athletes start to arrive through the gate, loose groups of four, or five, or six: They carry gym bags and are dressed in layers of T-shirts and fuzzy pants and sweat suits and hooded parkas of all colors. They talk quietly, smiling and joking a little. Collecting at the far end of the pool, they set down their bags and begin, still talking among themselves, to stretch up on their toes, to bend from side to side, to do a few sit-ups and toe touches, twisting their bodies, pulling out each other's arms, stretching out in all directions. A man wearing a long blue parka with the hood pushed back off his blond hair circulates slowly among them, talking with some, periodically suggesting the next exercise. He is six feet tall and stocky, a former high-school football player, a former college swimmer. His name is Terry.

The gate in the wrought-iron fence opens once again and a small, thin man walks in, quickly. The teenagers continue to stretch but fall silent and watch as he approaches down the deck. He is in his midthirties, slightly stooped, very lean and muscular, like a distance runner. When he reaches the stretching athletes, he says quietly, "All right, let's go." The sweat suits come off, the T-shirts, the warm-up pants, the socks and tennis shoes, layer after layer, revealing firm, well-muscled bodies. Each athlete is left wearing, one on top of another, two or three nylon swimsuits, cut for racing. They pick up their gear and walk barefoot to the side of the pool (they swim their practice across the pool; it is as wide as most are long) and, after adjusting their goggles, dive in, one following another, slipping quietly into the water as the fog continues to rise.

They would swim for two hours that morning and cover some nine thousand yards in the water—a little more than five miles. To build their arms they would pull themselves, with their legs hobbled by a rubber strap around the ankles, for a thousand yards—forty lengths; to strengthen their legs they would kick, holding a floating plastic board, another thousand yards; they would swim twenty-five full-speed hundred-yard sprints, then swim some three-hundreds, and on and on for two hours, all of it fast enough that you have to walk briskly alongside the pool to keep up. In the afternoon they would come back after a full day of school and, after starting with five hundred sit-ups, they would lift weights for an hour and then swim for another two and a half hours. They do this six days a week, fifty weeks a year.

These are the best swimmers in America. Some are the best in the world.

A few go on to win Olympic gold medals; most are just lost in the crowd. There are no guarantees. No one knows (though any visitor would have suspicions) which ones will be the winners, the media stars, and which will be the great, sudden, shocking failures. Despite all hints and foreshadowings and despite all past successes—collegiate titles, National Championships, American records, even world records—until the final races in the Olympics no one knows who will win those medals, who will be publicly recognized as the best in the world.

A freak automobile accident on the last day of the Olympic Trials, an ankle twisted running down the stairs at home, a shoulder dislocated because of trying to lift a few pounds too many on the Nautilus machine, a race started out a bit too fast to sustain the speed, a bad argument with a girlfriend the night before—any one of these or a thousand other mishaps and a decade of grueling work could end in sorrow, a towel wrapped around one's drooping head while the national anthem plays for someone else. For these athletes, competitive swimming holds out only the promise of more competitive swimming—always renewed challenges, to be faced and overcome.

Those who would become champions—and Olympic gold medalists are one example of that species—might differ from the others, but the difference is not metaphysical or mysterious. There is no secret technique that makes them swim faster, no supernatural "psych-up" that allows them to win close races. If they had "natural ability," it can be discovered only by looking at their performance, after the fact. They become champions by doing what needs to be done, by doing everything right, by concentrating on all the silly details that others overlook. What makes them champions is the knowledge—and the action following from that knowledge—that champions are only real people, not gods, and that all it takes to *be* a champion is to *do* what champions do.

This is the story of a coach and some swimmers, the sport in which they live, of what finally makes them great—and of the all-too-human quality of their greatness.

CHAMPIONS

PART I

1

Evolution of a Team

YEARS AGO, IN THE FALL OF 1963, BEFORE MANY OF THOSE swimmers at that early-morning California practice were even born, a ninth-grade boy named Mark Schubert at Firestone High School in Akron, Ohio, tried out for the school swimming team. He found the practices demanding, and he wasn't very good. He was cut from the team.

One year later, he came back; this time he made the team. He began to enjoy the training, and he pushed himself. Smaller than most of his teammates, he began lifting weights, working with stretch cords, doing sit-ups every day to build his body. He swam the breaststroke (there are four strokes in competitive swimming: the butterfly; the backstroke; the breaststroke; and the freestyle, which laypersons call "the crawl"), and by his senior year he was among the best breaststroke swimmers in Ohio. He enjoyed the training, the discipline of it, the order that swimming gave his life. He knew that mentally he was a champion.

But physically—because of his small size, and later because of serious injuries—he would never be a great swimmer. So he decided to coach.

Schubert spent the summers during his high-school years at the Fairlawn Country Club, helping to coach the swim team there, and lifeguarding at a different pool. When the team coach at that other pool quit, Mark took over the job. In charge for the first time, he began to share his growing ambitions with the swimmers on his team: *You can be good at this,* he told them. *If you win this meet,* he'd say, *I'll take you all to the amusement park. We'll throw a party. You can be good swimmers, You can be great swimmers.* Within a year, his team was locally undefeated; within two years it was the best team in northern Ohio and western Pennsylvania. More than a decade later, Schubert, by then the most successful coach in America, would remember that first team with a smile. "I guess I created some enthusiasm."

In the fall of 1967, with a swimming scholarship in hand, he enrolled at the University of Kentucky. Early in that first year, while running to a class, he slipped on the sidewalk, fell, and broke his leg. He never fully recovered; his swimming suffered. Increasingly, he directed his energies into coaching others. In his sophomore year, he worked three nights a week coaching a club team in the basement of a local girls' school, in a three-lane, fifteen-yard pool—a large bathtub, almost—in Versailles, Kentucky. In his junior year he decided to stop swimming himself, and his coach let him be an assistant for the University of Kentucky team to keep his scholarship; he still kept his job in the basement pool in Versailles. Mark Schubert knew then that he wanted to build a national-level team; and he knew then, as he seemed always to know, that he could do it.

By his senior year in college, coaching dominated Mark Schubert's life. He was the assistant coach for the university and worked at the same time with a local swim club and with the Versailles basement group—three jobs at once, three different pools. Schubert drove himself. That year, nine swimmers from the University of Kentucky team qualified for the National Collegiate Athletic Association (NCAA) Championships. Never before had the team done so well. Still only a college student, Schubert was already building a reputation.

In April 1971, as he was finishing his senior year at Kentucky, he was offered a job as swim coach and physical-education instructor at Cuyahoga Falls High School, near his hometown of Akron. The Cuyahoga Falls swim team—the Black Tigers, they called themselves—were archrivals of Schubert's old Firestone High School team.

Over the summer he wrote letters to all the swimmers on the team; he called meetings with the seniors, one of whom was a football player named Terry Stoddard, son of the high-school football coach. Wearing his Black Tigers football shirt, Stoddard and the others came to have dinner with the new swimming coach.

Schubert said to him, *You're not really going to play football, are you?*

Terry said, *Yeah, I'm playing football.*

Schubert thought a minute and said, *Well, you're going to resign as senior class president, aren't you?*

Terry said, *No.*

Schubert told him and the others, *You can't do everything. You have to decide if you want to be great swimmers or not. Think about it.*

The swimmers, Terry and his friends, did think about it. They were unsure whether Schubert was a great coach or just crazy. But they knew that they had to decide—to quit the team or to stay and give this man Schubert everything he asked of them.

They stayed. Schubert talked with them many more times that year. He told them that the state high-school meet was not all there was—there were bigger meets: regional and national. He told them, *You have to be more than high-school swimmers; you have to work out twice a day, you have to train year-round, you have to shave your body for meets, you have to swim against the fastest swimmers we can find.* One weekend he took them up to Ann Arbor, Michigan, to see the regional championships—they got out of school Thursday and Friday to go. Terry Stoddard's parents and the teachers didn't like that at all. *What is this Schubert fellow up to?* Then one day Schubert loaded his eight best swimmers into a borrowed station wagon. Three of them had to get in the back on top of the suitcases. They were literally lying on top of one another, legs all tangled up. They drove all the way from Cuyahoga Falls, Ohio, over to West Point, New York, to the U.S. Military Academy, so that they could watch the NCAA Swimming Championships, which that year was the fastest swimming meet in the world. Terry Stoddard got in the water during the breaks in the meet, pretended he was swimming in the NCAA Championships; he wrote down everybody's times in their events on his program. By the middle of the year back in Cuyahoga Falls he was thinking, *I want to get a college scholarship, I want to go to Nationals, I want to swim in the fastest meet in the world.* Schubert had shown Terry Stoddard goals higher than he had ever dreamed.

But Schubert's goals were too high for Cuyahoga Falls. The Parks and Recreation Department, which controlled the pools, wanted a swimming team, but they also wanted a recreation program, and when the team wanted the pool for practices they were often turned down—the competitive program was getting to be a bit much for some people's taste. The way this Schubert was doing things, his team was starting to overshadow everything else. He was talking about building a new pool, just for the team. He had a kid on his team, a breaststroker named Jerry Hagel, whose father, John, was an architect. Schubert got together with John Hagel and together they drew up a set of blueprints for Schubert's dream facility. It would be a huge long lake of a pool, a true fifty-meter "Olympic size," over half the length of a football field, with a plastic bubble overhead so the team could swim all year long without having to rent separate training facilities. Schubert figured that somehow he'd borrow the money to build it. But that plan was a bit much for some people. The director of parks and recreation called Schubert in and said, in a friendly enough way, *You know, Mark, someday you're going to be a great coach, but it's never going to be in Cuyahoga Falls.*

Schubert went home, thought about that, and decided that the director was right. The next week he wrote some letters applying for jobs in California, where people took swimming a little more seriously.

Competitive swimming changed rapidly in the late 1960s and early 1970s, and Mark Schubert was ready to exploit those changes. His team would be (although he couldn't have known it then) a new kind: tightly organized, financed by corporate wealth, fed by athletes imported from across the United States and around the world, and dominated by an untouchable coach. This would be a far cry from the days of Johnny Weismuller and Buster Crabbe, of the 1920s and 1930s, a long way from the casual organization of the 1948 Olympic swim team in which the women were issued one blouse, one shirt, two skirts—and had no laundry service. There was about to occur a dramatic shift away from the country-club-league and leisure-time mentality that had characterized swimming in America throughout the 1950s and early 1960s, into a highly rational pursuit of a human being's physical limits.

There were interesting reasons for this change. Beginning in the late 1950s, a swimming coach named James E. (later called "Doc") Counsilman from Indiana University, working for an M.S. and a Ph.D. in kinesiology (physical education), began experimental studies of the breaststroke and, later, of the flutter kick used in freestyle swimming. He filmed swimmers from underwater, did stop-action analyses, drew force diagrams, and ran strength tests of muscles in different positions. From his findings he significantly modified the breaststroke and helped a young swimmer named Chet Jastremski (who could not even float unaided) to drop the world record in the hundred-meter breaststroke by four seconds. Counsilman's book *The Science of Swimming*, published in 1968, went far beyond the other swimming manuals of its time—sophisticated, scientific, clear, and practical, it revolutionized the study of technique in swimming.

Around the same time—in the early 1960s—a former World War II pilot named Sherm Chavoor, who owned the Arden Hills Tennis Club near Sacramento, used the pool there to give a small group of swimmers the hardest workouts he could dream up. In an era when most national-level swimmers were training for one and a half to three hours a day, Chavoor put his people in the water three times a day for a total of five hours daily. They swam workouts far beyond anything such 1964 Olympic stars as Don Schollander or Donna DeVarona ever did, swam more miles in a day than many distance runners ran. Their workouts continued, often, until the athletes literally collapsed of exhaustion.

Chavoor built his program around a few incredible swimmers. One of them was Mike Burton. Burton, at the age of fourteen, had been in a motorcycle accident and had been told he couldn't run anymore and couldn't play football. So the boy tried swimming. Every day Burton would limp to the pool on his bad leg. Humble and eager, Burton willingly subjected himself to a training regimen that many coaches described as "sick." (Doc Counsilman more generously described Burton as one of the hardest-working athletes of all time, an "agonist" who seemed to enjoy causing himself pain.) The truth is, Burton was by his own admission very ambitious; and with a stroke so choppy that it caused traditional coaches to wince, he demolished the world records in the distance freestyle events. Debby Meyer, his very tough sixteen-year-old Arden Hills teammate, did the same in the women's events. Between them they took six gold medals at the Mexico City Olympics in 1968, and the swimming world adopted wholesale the concept of "overdistance training," which basically meant swimming long distances with short rest intervals. Across the United States, coaches began giving their athletes long workouts swimming freestyle and butterfly, developing programs that for the first time challenged their physical limits. Many fine athletes simply couldn't do it; their bodies broke down under the punishment. Andy Strenk, a 1968 Olympian, went to Arden Hills in 1972 to train with Chavoor in order to make the team again. Three weeks before the Olympic Trials, he went home and fell asleep. When he awoke and tried to stand up, he fell to the floor and crawled, hands and knees, to the bathroom. He managed to go to the Trials but was ruined; he didn't make the team. The grueling training, made possible in part by the introduction of goggles so swimmers wouldn't go blind spending five hours a day in chlorinated water, drove many people out of the sport. But world records, especially in the longer endurance events, continued to fall.

Finally, changes within the United States as a whole affected swimming. The population in the 1970s was shifting to the Sunbelt, where there were more pools and warmer weather, where swimmers could train outdoors year-round. And the women's movement brought scholarships for college women's programs, so that women who earlier might have left the sport now stayed in for four more years.

As a result of all this—the technical improvements (as exemplified in Counsilman's work), the more rigorous training programs (as practiced by Chavoor), and the social and demographic shifts—the swimmers of the 1980s became much faster than the swimmers of the 1960s. The former were stronger, they had more endurance, their strokes were somewhat better, their coaches were more knowledgeable, the pools these athletes swam in were faster (with antiturbulence lane dividers and deeper water to reduce waves)— and times in all events dropped drastically. Times that were world records in the early 1960s would, by the early 1980s, not even qualify a swimmer to enter the U.S. National Championships.

On Memorial Day weekend in late May 1972, Mark Schubert flew out to California and interviewed for five different coaching jobs. He was offered four of them. One was in Orange County, about an hour south of Los Angeles on the San Diego Freeway, where the Mission Viejo Company—which later that year would become part of the Philip Morris Corporation—was building and selling thousands of houses, a planned development community, south of Irvine on the site of the old Rancho de Mission Viejo. The company was putting together a recreation program for the community and wanted an aquatics director. He would have virtually unlimited pool time in several pools; the program was to be organized however he wanted. There would be a fifty-meter competition pool, and the new director would have a hand in its design. Schubert took the job.

He asked for one special clause in his contract: that the Mission Viejo Company pay all travel and hotel expenses for any swimmer making the National Championships. This was in June 1972; Schubert was twenty-three years old, one year out of college. At that time, no swimmer from Mission Viejo had ever made the cut-off times for Nationals. The team pointed its season toward the Orange County (CA) Championships. So the company people said, *Sure, sounds like a great deal. Where do we sign?* They could hardly have known what they were getting into.

In return, they wanted a family-oriented recreational swimming program with a place for everyone, and—importantly—a classy operation. Schubert shaved off his moustache and put his blue jeans back in the drawer in order to project a more "professional" image. The teams he coached would also look good. Their sweat suits were made of heavy material, nicely designed and clean. Their appearance in public was to be wholesome. In this respect Schubert would succeed magnificently and would be proud of the influence his team's appearance was to have on others in the sport. As he saw it, coaches were not beach bums, and they shouldn't look it. He wanted to look—and *be*—better than anyone else.

Schubert went to Mission Viejo with the clear vision he had had since college, of winning the AAU (Amateur Athletic Union) National Swimming Championships team title. Twice a year, the AAU held a National Championship meet. One was held in the spring, indoors in a twenty-five-yard pool. The other, in late summer, was in a fifty-meter pool, the international standard. Participants came from the over two thousand AAU-sanctioned competitive swim clubs around the country. Here was the cream of the some 150,000 registered competitive swimmers in the United States. In the late 1970s, following legal rulings that shook the AAU, the entire swimming organization would secede from the AAU and form its own governing body to be called U.S. Swimming, which would continue holding the Nationals. There were also, of course, high school and collegiate competitions, but for Schubert what mattered was AAU competition, the club sport, where swimmers trained with one team the entire year and swam in international competitions, with the ultimate goal of the Olympic Games. Now he had the resources, he thought, to win that title: financial backing, magnificent facilities, unlimited time in the water, and a huge population of swimmers in the Los Angeles area.

He spent the first summer in Mission Viejo laying the foundations. He banned parents from workouts. He refused excuses for missing practice. He locked the gates so latecomers couldn't get in. He allowed no illegal strokes or sloppy turns in practices; you had to do things right, all the time. He drove his swimmers relentlessly, and years later they would remember how he walked back and forth the length of the pool for hours on end, bent over the water, screaming his lungs out. They did unbelievable workouts, perhaps more strenuous than anyone in the world had ever done before. Three or four times a week, Mark Schubert, furious with imperfections of technique, with failures of effort, would explode into a rage. Many swimmers quit the team; some hated him. Schubert's temper hurt him, too; it was bad for him physically and psychologically. He would learn over the years to tone it down, and it became more of a staged technique. But that first summer, and for several years afterward, his emotional volatility was genuine, and it would become—for a time, at least—his trademark. Ten years later, some of those original Mission Viejo swimmers would find that when they talked with him, even over the telephone, their hands trembled.

Parents in Mission Viejo wondered, as Terry Stoddard's had back in Cuyahoga Falls, *What is Schubert up to?* Forbidden to watch practices, they had nowhere to direct their enthusiasm. When the team won the Orange County dual meet title that first year, a Mission Viejo Company executive vice president whose daughter was on the team suggested it would be fun to throw the coach—Schubert—into the pool as a little celebration. Schubert responded that no one would be thrown in until after the conference championship meet. The parents were put off, but Schubert had established himself as the boss.

Some parents wanted him fired. They believed he had

orchestrated the ouster of the former coach—who, in fact, was one of his friends. They pulled their children off the team. They complained bitterly among themselves. But he had a contract, and he worked for the Mission Viejo Company, not the parents. The company executives liked the way Schubert did business. They gave him free rein; and he ran a program with opportunities for everyone, from the novice to the—he hoped—potential Olympic champion. The executives had never dreamed that the Mission Viejo Nadadores ("swimmers" in Spanish) could win the National Championships. If they had, they might not have hired a twenty-three-year-old nobody from Ohio.

Now that Schubert had a team, a pool, and a vision, he began teaching swimmers how to go fast. He found that often people set their sights very low. The parents, especially, felt that with the Orange County Championships the team had won it all. In the beginning, Schubert didn't tell the parents or the kids of his national aspirations, for fear of scaring them away. But he gradually raised their sights: He told them, as he had told the swimmers back in Cuyahoga Falls, of tougher workouts, faster times, bigger meets, and greater victories.

In the fall of that first year, 1972, Schubert called the team together and announced that he was starting a senior training program designed to help swimmers make the National Championships. They would train twice a day, six or seven days each week, year-round; they would lift weights, and they would swim very, very hard. Again many of them quit, but those who stayed kept swimming faster.

A month later Peggy Tosdal, who had retired from swimming six months earlier, after the Olympic Trials, came out of retirement to swim at Mission with Schubert. By April 1973, Schubert took Tosdal and three other girls to the Nationals in Cincinnati. Tosdal swam in the hundred-yard butterfly, and she finished second, to the surprise of everyone. Tosdal previously had never finished higher than fifth.

On Sunday morning, the last day of the National Championships that spring, Terry Stoddard was lying in bed in his dorm room at Eastern Kentucky University, eighty miles south of Cincinnati. The phone rang. It was Mark Schubert, Terry's old swim coach from Cuyahoga Falls High School, calling. Terry came to the phone.

Why aren't you here? asked Schubert.

Where? said Stoddard.

Cincinnati, at Nationals.

Well, said Terry, *I just didn't know much about it. I guess I didn't have a ride. . . .*

Schubert didn't want Terry just to come to watch the meet; he also wanted Terry and the other guys from Cuyahoga Falls to come out to Mission Viejo, live there for the summer, and train to swim in Nationals. Schubert said he would find homes for them, and he talked their parents into it. In May 1973, Terry Stoddard and most of the guys from the team went out to Mission Viejo. Schubert gave them all T-shirts that read "Think Nationals" on the back, and they started swimming between eighteen thousand and twenty thousand meters a day—eight miles. For seven days a week—twenty-one straight days at one point—they did two workouts a day. Schubert knew that there was that clause in his contract; and he told them, with a wink, that he'd made this special deal with the Mission Viejo Company, and that if they made Nationals, he'd *fly* them home—because the Nationals were in Louisville, Kentucky.

That year, nine swimmers from Mission Viejo qualified for the Louisville Summer Nationals, and Peggy Tosdal, in finishing second, made the World Championship team from the United States. Schubert's program was beginning to pay off.

Schubert went to the World Championships in Belgrade, Yugoslavia, that year to watch Peggy Tosdal swim. For more than a decade afterward the meet would be called simply "Belgrade"; it marked a turning point in international swimming, the arrival of East Germany as the dominant power in women's swimming.

The press called the East German women the *Wundermädchen*—Supergirls. They were huge, some of them over six feet tall, and so muscular that their appearance provoked rumors of steroid use. More importantly, they were incredibly fast. They dominated the women's events, smashing world records and humiliating an American team that still carried the memories of Donna DeVarona in the 1964 Tokyo Olympics and Debby Meyer in 1968 in Mexico City. Now these German heroines of the proletariat were demolishing the old records and challenging traditional standards of feminine beauty at the same time.

They wore "skin suits," racing suits of a single layer of stretch nylon. Skin suits had first appeared internationally at the 1972 Olympics on an Italian girl named Novella Calligaris, who won a silver medal in the four-hundred-meter freestyle. American television had shown her from the neck up only, and the American commentator—Donna DeVarona—said the suit appeared to be "glued on." Press reporters called the suits provocative and revealing; but Calligaris swam fast wearing one in 1972, and then she broke the world record in the eight hundred the next year. People noticed. Schubert noticed. He came back from Belgrade and ordered European skin suits for his team. The Mission Viejo Nadadores would be the first team in America to wear them.

The winter season of 1973–74 was an exciting one as the Nadadores, inspired by Tosdal's performance, trained hard and as still more new swimmers came to the team, many of them from the recently disbanded Huntington Beach Aquatics Club, to which Tosdal had belonged. Shirley Babashoff, the best woman swimmer of the mid-1970s, was probably the most notable of these. Schubert took twenty-two swimmers to the winter Nationals that year, and Mission Viejo's women finished second, by about fifty points, to the Santa Clara Swim Club.

Evolution of a Team

That summer it was closer, and the victory was in doubt right down until the final day of the meet. But the women's team won. Over the next eleven years, with two championship meets a year, and three titles—men's, women's, and combined—available at each meet, Mission Viejo would win forty-four titles. They would dominate the sport as no other team in history.

In two years, from 1972 to 1974, Mark Schubert had taken the Mission Viejo Nadadores from the Orange County Swim Conference, which they had never won, to winning the National Team Championships. In 1974 he coached the most powerful swimming team in America. He was only twenty-five years old.

2

The Master Planner

SCHUBERT'S EXPERIENCE, WHILE EXEMPLARY, IS NOT UNIQUE; great swimming coaches rise quickly. James E. "Doc" Counsilman, who wrote The Science of Swimming, coached an Olympic champion in 1948, his second year in the profession. Don Gambril, who would head the U.S. Olympic staff in 1984, had an Olympian, Sharon Stouder, within two years of beginning his coaching career. None of these coaches were initially experts on the techniques of swimming or the physiology of exercise.

It seems that coaches choose their level of achievement by choosing their level of expectations. Information is not a problem. Books are available that tell what one needs to do: this type of organization, that type of workout, these stroke-and-turn techniques. Counsilman's book gave information not only on strokes but also on training, diet, calisthenics and weightlifting, even the motivation of athletes. Recently a coach named Ernie Maglischo has written

Swimming Faster, a sort of 1980s version of Counsilman's book, updating all the scientific research on fluid mechanics and exercise physiology.

There are journal articles, too, that answer every conceivable technical question, and if you come up with an inconceivable question, there are coaches' clinics in various locations around the country all year long, so you can pay thirty dollars to hear a famous coach lecture, then ask him your question afterward. There are dozens of local-level coaches at those clinics, all sitting there frantically taking notes, peering intently at charts and slides and films, asking about stroke drills and motivational methods. A few of them, perhaps, might think, *These guys don't know anything special.* They are right in a sense: There is no special knowledge.

The difference, what makes Schubert and a few others remarkable, is not their knowledge, not something that could be learned from a book, symposium, or clinic, but simply their willingness to *do* what is necessary. All the "little" things Schubert began in his first summer at Mission mattered. Schubert knew that the swimmers should be on time for workouts—if for no other reason than to confirm their commitment to the team. He knew that swimmers needed to practice doing turns according to the rules, so kids who didn't do their turns properly were pulled out of the pool to do push-ups. At major meets, swimmers should go to bed early, so Schubert would go from room to room, checking beds. He wanted them to eat a balanced diet, so Schubert had the team's meals catered, and he designed the menu. He told them what suits to wear and what caps to wear (for instance, for a long event in an outdoor meet never wear a black cap—it absorbs heat and makes you tired). For years he forbade the swimmers from going to the bathroom during practice, since time was lost. Now, less strict, he expects only that if they go, they run to the dressing room and back. He writes workouts that reflect his knowledge of physiology and that assume his swimmers *want* to be great; his workouts challenge the body and mind to their limits. Rather than make accommodations for the weaker swimmers, the less dedicated, he gears everything to the champions and toward anyone who wants to be like them.

His method is simple. He sees clearly what he wants to accomplish, and he brooks no interference. This makes him unpopular with the less committed athletes (who feel driven) and sometimes even frightening to those whose goals are not as high as his. This is not to say that he is obsessed with swimming (he is not) or that he is unpleasant to less serious athletes (not at all). But within the Senior Nationals team, his elite group, he assumes total dedication, and the athlete who falls short of that standard soon discovers that he or she simply doesn't belong there.

Many people say that Schubert is authoritarian, and they speak of a sadistic impulse or psychological need to dominate. Sharply critical—even personally vicious—articles were written, during the late 1970's, about him and his program at Mission Viejo. They mistook the strict discipline for an almost inhuman obsession with winning and with the systematic destruction of children's personalities. Schubert himself, aware of those comments, speaks jokingly of his "German ancestry," aware of his tightly regimented, almost moralistic approach to the organization of his swimming team. His is the final word on everything, no doubt of that.

But to call him authoritarian, or to refer to his program as a "factory," or a "machine," as many people do, is not to explain how he does it. One must first come to know the emotional intensity of workouts. Here are a mass of people pressed closely together, day in and day out, for hours each day; all the athletes are nearly naked and in almost constant pain, working for goals that are tremendously important to them, and working with others through long, tedious, almost ritualistic routines. Some of the comparisons are obvious: military boot camp, ascetic practices of some religious sects, transcendental meditation. Imagine five hours a day staring at a line on the bottom of a swimming pool.

They do this for years on end, five hours a day, literally at Schubert's feet. Standing at the focus of all this physical and emotional energy, Mark Schubert plays it like a piano; he is a master of the art. He *stands* on the deck above the swimmers; they are below him in the water. While some coaches—Eddie Reese of the University of Texas, or his brother Randy of the University of Florida, for instance—will sometimes sit on a starting block at the end of the pool, or squat down on the pool deck to talk with a swimmer, Schubert always stands when talking to them during a workout. In his office—the only place where he receives negative comments on the program from swimmers—he seats his guests on a sofa before the conversation begins, and they find that their seat is a bit lower than his (he didn't plan it that way, but it is true nevertheless). When talking with swimmers on the pool deck during a meet, he usually comes close, within five or six inches. His sharp hazel-green eyes cut right into you. Unless one is ready to accept what he says, it's much too close for comfort. It puts you in a tough spot: He stands right up in your face and says, *You can win this race. You can set a world record.* If you can stand there, with this man telling you this, right in your face, his eyes never drifting, his voice clear and direct, you start, they say, to believe what he is saying.

His looks can vary: a little bit of laughter at the edges, or disgust, or quick anger. His swimmers learn to read those looks. Smaller than most of his swimmers (even the women), he overwhelms many of them by the sheer force of his personality and an aggressive use of "body language." He uses his eyes, his hands, his stance on the deck like an actor or a singer. He approaches each workout, as he himself says, "like a performance." And if workouts are his performance, then the Marguerite Recreation Center is his theater.

Like many top coaches, he prefers workouts to meets—by the time the meets come around, the coach's job is largely done. In the final analysis, swimming is an individual sport: One person wins or loses, and despite the fact that team scores are kept, no teamwork is necessary during the competition. At meets the coach becomes a side figure—true also in tennis, in golf, and in gymnastics. In such team sports as football, basketball, and baseball, the coach matters more and has more power. But the swimming coach uses his power in the workouts. That's where the training is done, where the confidence is built.

By 1983 Schubert's coaching style had changed since the early years. His temper has subsided. In 1973 it was frightening; by 1983 he had "mellowed a lot," according to some of the former swimmers who came to visit now and then. Other coaches noticed it, too: Ron O'Brien, the Olympic diving coach who worked in the next pool, said time and again that Schubert had calmed down in just the past few years. Paul Asmuth, the world champion professional marathon swimmer, in his late twenties, who swam for Schubert years before, could see it; Jennifer Hooker, an Olympic team member from 1980, could see it. Schubert himself feels better for having relaxed.

In part, the change was simply maturation. During his years as an assistant coach at the University of Kentucky, he had worked for a head coach who was very young, only three years older than Schubert himself. Schubert had seen the problems of coaching athletes close to one's own age. So when he came to Mission as a twenty-three-year-old, he was always very concerned to *draw the line,* in his own phrase; he was trying to earn their respect that way. His reputation was built on those years, from 1973 through 1976 or 1977, when he coached such gold medalists as

Brian Goodell; and then in the late 1970s, when many of the best distance swimmers in the world—Steve Holland, or Casey Converse, or Jesse Vassallo—would come and train at Mission.

Perhaps he was becoming more reflective. He was growing older anyway, and was more secure in his abilities as a coach, less anxious about proving something. His swimmers had already won numerous national titles and a handful of Olympic medals; he had already been Coach of the Year. But it was really the 1980 boycott of the Moscow Games by the United States that forced him to think about what he had been doing and what he wanted to do. Years later he would remember sitting in a hotel room in Washington, D.C., waiting to go out with the U.S. Olympic Team (of which he was a coach) and meet with President Carter, who would try to explain why there would be no Olympics for this team. It had been a depressing summer, a sobering year, watching all the hard work and planning frustrated. These kids had worked so hard, only to be disappointed; all the discipline and drive and ambition was cut off in midstream. Yet he realized, as he sat there in his hotel room, that the Olympics weren't everything; there was the joy of constantly striving to be better, to be as good as you can be. *It's too bad,* he thought, *that we aren't going to the Olympics, but there's always next time. There are other meets. You don't need the Olympics to feel like you're doing something worthwhile.* At that point Mark Schubert really began to enjoy coaching.

One event in particular would come to exemplify for Schubert his new attitude and evolving sense of purpose. Normally he would not attend the National Junior Olympics, the "Junior Nationals" where the best eighteen-year-old and younger swimmers came to compete if they didn't qualify for the Nationals. His assistant Larry Liebowitz ran the Mission Junior Nationals team, and Schubert never interfered. But in 1983 Schubert had a swimmer at Juniors who had failed to make the Nationals cutoff, a high schooler named Vic Riggs. So Schubert went to Juniors to see Riggs swim. At the meet, held in Brown Deer, Wisconsin, Vic Riggs swam terrifically, breaking his own best time in the five-hundred-yard freestyle by a healthy bit and winning the event. Schubert felt then, and for years to come, that Riggs' race was as exciting to him, as fulfilling, as Brian Goodell's breaking the world record years before, or Shirley Babashoff's gold medal in 1976, or all the National Team Championships, as exciting as anything he'd ever seen; he'd worked for years with Riggs and knew that this boy had deserved to win. Schubert loved telling the story of that race and of his own reaction to it. He was proud that he was a coach who enjoyed that.

He no longer loses control, nor does he need to. Mark Schubert now exhibits the quiet of a man who claims the respect of every swimmer on his team. Because the swimmers rarely challenge him, he need hardly ever show anger—only once every few months, and even then it is, he says, contrived, a bit of a show just to keep everybody in line. He now speaks to the swimmers with a careful courtesy: *I'd like the ladies in lanes one through five, the gentlemen in lanes six through ten. . . . Let's start in fifteen seconds, please.* When he can't quite hear a question, he says, *Pardon me?* When asked to allow an exception to a rule (a twenty-five-year-old asked if he could have wine with dinner after Nationals) he says, *I'd rather you didn't.* No one at Mission Viejo mistakes this courtesy for weakness: Schubert's requests are orders. With his reputation, Mark Schubert can afford to be gracious. He entertains his swimmers at his home, he takes them out water skiing, he talks with them as friends.

By 1983, the year before the Los Angeles Olympic Games, his authority was completely taken for granted. Having had great swimmers, he attracted others who wanted to become great and were willing to pay the price:

The Master Planner

hence more great swimmers. With as many as one hundred to two hundred applications for twenty-five to thirty available places on his senior team each summer, he could choose the best. Having added the best to his team, his and the team's reputation grew larger. They believed he could make them great, and often they did become great. The power of the team was self-perpetuating, and Schubert was the center of that power.

He still controlled the pools through his relationship with the company, which had profited far more from the team than its executives could have imagined. When the swimming team became national champions, one of the executives in the company thought a diving team would be nice, too, so he hired the man whom many thought was the best diving coach in the world, Ron O'Brien, and built him a beautiful diving pool. Schubert had even raised the company's ambitions.

Schubert also established himself in the organizational hierarchy of U.S. Swimming. For several years he served as U.S.S. Technical Vice President, and was a member of the rules committee as well. He formed connections with a number of college coaches and regularly sent athletes to Southern Methodist University, UCLA, and USC, among others—and those college coaches returned the athletes to him in the summertime. He built at Mission Viejo an organization of parents, secretaries, local swimming volunteers, public officials in Mission Viejo, travel agents, public-relations people, and local and regional media; he built strong working relationships with the local high schools—by coaching there in the early years and later by placing his assistant coaches as teachers in the schools. He also provided the high-school teams with instant success through his housing program for visiting stars from around the world. His team was the best advertisement the town of Mission Viejo had ever had. Every time swimmer Tiffany Cohen appeared in *People* magazine, or in *Sports Illus-*

trated; every time diver Greg Louganis appeared on the *Tonight* show with Johnny Carson, or in *Life* magazine, the name of Mission Viejo was there, and the Mission Viejo Company knew that such national publicity was irreplaceable.

Many coaches called the Mission Viejo Nadadores "The best swimming team money can buy," with its lavish facilities, the free equipment given all swimmers the day they arrive, the travel and hotel expenses that few other teams can offer. But in the end, the financial support had to be organized, too—and Schubert did that by talking to community groups and cajoling company executives, wheedling support, and organizing booster clubs. Yet money alone could not buy athletic success. It was up to Schubert to put the money to good use; it was Schubert who gave the organization a purpose. His success was greater, in some sense, than that of the Mission Viejo Company itself.

He was a master planner and an organizer. His ambition was not to be a great coach but to have a great program, a great team. As a result of his organizational talents, he has been remarkably successful as a swimming coach and lives better than most coaches, as well as the parents of his athletes. He resides in a home overlooking the beach on Lake Mission Viejo, with a pool on the deck. He drives over to the Marguerite Recreation Center in the morning in his BMW (he also favors Porsches); his car has vanity plates ("Schubs"), and his Land's End luggage is monogrammed ("MES"). His salary is not public, but in an occupation where the average annual salary may be twenty thousand dollars, most estimates put his at somewhere over a hundred thousand dollars a year.

Although he has always worked hard—how many thirty-five-year-olds will climb out of bed every morning at four-thirty just to stand over a swimming pool for two hours?—he is not obsessed with swimming. In 1983 he spent twenty-eight days skiing; he has run in the New York Marathon; he enjoys cycling and water skiing. He can see coaching for the rest of his life—"helping kids accomplish their goals," as he says, and doing all right for himself besides.

PART II

PART II

3

California Dreaming

A VISITOR TO CALIFORNIA HAS NO TROUBLE FINDING MISSION
Viejo. You arrive at Los Angeles International Airport,
climb into your rent-a-car, and drive south on the freeway
past used-car lots, past the sprawling oil refineries of Long
Beach, past oil tankers at the docks, past countless gas stations and Toyota dealerships, down the seventy miles of
San Diego Freeway along with thousands of other cars, all
going seventy miles an hour through the once-desert valley
where hundreds of migrant workers are hunched over
picking lettuce, past the El Toro Marine Air Base where
jets swoop down low over the freeways, south toward San
Diego. Seventy miles down the long valley come the five
exits for Mission Viejo—"the California Promise," as a
large billboard announces it.

You turn off the freeway and cruise onto La Paz Parkway, to find hundreds and hundreds of low stucco houses
spread over the hills of Orange County amid neatly

trimmed lawns and "green spaces" laid out in carefully planned variety along the roads. There are no billboards here in Mission Viejo; no trash, no golden arches, no tall trees or tall buildings, just hundreds of low red and brown stucco houses along curving streets with such Spanish names as El Toro, Alicante, Marguerite.

Normally no one in Mission Viejo talks about the weather—the sun is always there, and it is always hot. But in January 1983, people did talk about the weather, because it was unusual. It was cold for January, the temperature dipping into the thirties at night, climbing up only into the fifties during the day. On Monday morning, January 31, 1983, the wind was blowing across the deck of the Olympic-size swimming pool at the Marguerite Recreation Center so hard that as the swimmers of Mark Schubert's Senior Nationals team went down the pool, their splashes landed three lanes over, twenty feet away. A thick fog blanketed the water, so that the swimmers at the far end were almost hidden from view. The mountains around Mission Viejo were capped with snow and shrouded by clouds.

The swimmers of the Mission Viejo Senior Nationals team, the top group of elite swimmers in America, were pulling themselves down the pool, their ankles bound with rubber tubes, floating buoys between their legs, their hands wrapped by large plastic paddles—all to put tremendous stress on the arm muscles. Their coach (Schubert's assistant), Scott MacFarland, sat watching on a folding metal chair. He was bundled up in hunting boots, two pairs of pants, a long-sleeved pullover shirt, and a hooded rain parka, with a scarf around his face and with gloves on his hands. In the summers he wears track shorts and glacier glasses, but now he hunkered down in his chair as the swimmers did laps for two hours. Mark Schubert, with ten of the best swimmers on the team, was in West Germany for the week, and Scott had been left in charge.

From five-thirty to seven-thirty in the morning the Senior team swam nine thousand yards; in the afternoon they came back at three o'clock and, after the usual five hundred sit-ups—some conventional, some with twenty-five-pound weights on their chests, some with a partner trying to hold them down—they lifted weights for an hour in the "Nadadores' Strength Room." The weight room is futuristic, something like a Victoria Principal Health Spa with Fruit Bar. Mirrors line the walls, carpet covers the floor, and scattered about are Universal gyms, Mini-Gyms, Biokinetic Swim Benches, free weights, pulley weights, surgical tubing stations, pneumatic press machines, dumbbells and barbells and, high on the back wall, a timer with a horn to signal when to start and when to stop each exercise. The athletes went through their circuits, spending perhaps a minute on each machine, then took a brief rest and on to the next machine; then around the circuit again, and once more before heading out to the pool to stretch and swim. Starting at four o'clock they swam for two and a half hours, another nine thousand yards or so. In a typical day they burn more calories than many Americans burn in a week; in a year they swim more than three million yards. They stop only five or ten seconds between swims; and they rest maybe a minute or two between "sets" of swims, just long enough to allow the heart rate to fall to where it will hurt to push it back up again, long enough to check the clock around which the entire practice is organized. All around the pool there are the clocks: a large electronic scoreboard clock visible from fifty meters away; sweep-second pacing clocks at every corner; hand-carried digital pace clocks that the coaches move from lane to lane; stopwatches stuffed in coaches' pockets. Mark Schubert always carries two or three stopwatches.

The training itself appears, to visitors, incredibly monotonous. The athletes swim their hundreds of laps by following the black line on the pool bottom, with two or three people in a lane swimming in an elongated oval, always

staying on the right-hand side of the lane to avoid colli-
sions. Yet strangely they seem to find it exhilarating, re-
freshing somehow. For hours you can get away from the
real world, from any other problems. For hours there is
only the water and the air, one's own body and the pain.
Those who swim the longer distances especially are often
very thoughtful and quiet when they talk about it, like the
ascetics who practice yoga or transcendental meditation.

Sometimes one of the swimmers, at the finish of a long
set, would catapult out of the water and, steam rising from
his wet back, charge to the locker room to go to the
bathroom. Within a minute, he would charge back out and
dive in the pool to continue swimming.

The Marguerite Recreation Center pool itself (there are
five other pools for the team in Mission Viejo), used by the
Senior National team and the Junior National team, is
twenty-five yards wide and fifty meters long, so that both
short- (twenty-five-yard) and long-course (fifty-meter) races
can be held there. Off one end of the pool is a separate
diving pool, 25 yards by 25 meters and 16 feet deep. It has
an Olympic diving tower with platforms at 5, 7½, and 10
meters, several boards, mirrors, spotting equipment for
gymnastics and landing pits for practicing flips. Under all
the diving platforms hang signs reading "Mission Viejo."
There are competition starting platforms down the length
of the pool, and under every one hangs a yellow and blue
"Mission Viejo" sign. The grounds, not much larger than
the pool itself (land is expensive in Orange County) are
planted with gardens, so in the springtime the air smells
not of chlorine, but of flowers. The grass is neatly mown,
the shrubs trimmed, the pennants which stretch across the
pool are smartly hung with the excess cord coiled tight
(Schubert liked that). Lane lines, to mark one lane from the
next and reduce wave turbulence, are blue and yellow;
kickboards for practice are blue and yellow; team suits are
blue and yellow, as are warmup suits and T-shirts, and

even towels. In a flower bed three feet wide and twenty-five feet long, on the slope overlooking the pool, in red flowers are written the words "Mission Viejo." On Schubert's door there is a (blue and yellow) sign: "Mission Viejo isn't everything, it's the only thing."

The swimmers in the pool look average. The girls are a bit taller than their classmates at school, most about five-seven or five-eight but ranging from five to perhaps six feet. Both girls and boys are very lean, with well-defined muscles. The average body fat percentage for girls at Mission Viejo High is probably 20 to 25 percent; among the girls on the team it's more like 15 percent. For the boys, the body fat percentage is still lower. Most of these kids have stiff, greenish-blond hair. Bleached out by the chlorinated water, it's very distinctive.

They speak the usual California lingo, share the usual jokes, enjoy many of the usual foods (although they forgo some); they talk about movies, the beach, magazines, hair-styles, boys and girls. Swimming takes six hours a day—but that still leaves eighteen. You can see them Friday night at movie theaters, at shopping malls, at the beach, at cookouts. On tour, they play video games in the hotel. They are not "serious" all the time.

If they are antisocial or socially backward, as some would stereotype them, it certainly doesn't show here. If anything, they are more outgoing than their peers, more comfortable with adults. They have a circle of friends—mainly other swimmers, since that is how they spend so much time. And they have friends not only from nearby, but also from across the country and even from around the world. Major swim meets are intensely social events, with lots of hellos all around, joking and laughing, cheering for pals and favorites. There are pats on the back, handshakes and hugs with competitors after almost all the races. At meets reporters often find it nearly impossible to find an athlete who is not already talking with someone else—a friend, coach, reporter, fan, whomever. But these kids are remarkable. Those who win national championships or set world records or win at the Olympics will know many people they would otherwise never meet, travel to places most people have never seen, push themselves past limits others believe impassable, and suffer disappointments that most of us would find staggering.

On the cold winter day of 1983, one could stand and look at the swimmers in the Marguerite pool and see some hopefuls for the 1984 Olympic Games, mainly among the distance swimmers. The Mission team was always known for distance swimmers who did the long, long workouts at nearly top speed, mile after mile. At the National Championships, Mission gets its points in the distance freestyle and distance stroke events, like the four-hundred-meter individual medley, in which the swimmer does a hundred meters (two lengths of a fifty-meter pool) of each of the four competitive strokes; or like the two-hundred-meter butterfly, roughly one eighth of a mile. In the shorter stroke events there are some finals in which they have no one entered. Mission Viejo stars over the years, from Shirley Babashoff and Brian Goodell to Casey Converse and Paul Asmuth and Jesse Vassallo and Tiffany Cohen were all great distance swimmers. Schubert planned it that way, knowing that it was easier to take young swimmers with less natural talent and less muscle and train them to make the National cutoff times in the distance events, where courage and hard work count for more than size and power. Distance swimming is the most reliable way to score points at Nationals, and Schubert considered it the best reflection of a coach and a program; the sprints were more the measure of a particular swimmer, of raw natural talent. He knew that natural ability—the feel for the water, size, hormones, and percentage of fast-twitch muscle—

play a role in swimming success. During his career he had coached national champions in all four strokes and in all distances, sprints as well as the longer events. But he would rather build on those natural talents, or better yet make great swimmers from kids without those advantages. One of Schubert's goals since he started at Mission in 1973 was to have his swimmers win both of the Olympic distance events, the men's fifteen-hundred freestyle (a "metric mile" of crawl) and the women's eight-hundred freestyle. In 1976 his swimmers had nearly achieved that, as Brian Goodell won the fifteen hundred, the longest event for men, and Shirley Babashoff took second in the eight hundred, the longest for women.

The favorite in 1983 to make the Olympic team (and perhaps to win the women's eight-hundred free) was Tiffany Cohen. She was seventeen years old, a high school junior, five feet, nine inches tall with long arms and a large head resting on broad shoulders. She had won several national championships. She might walk in to practice wearing Australian National team warm-ups, the result perhaps of a trade, or carrying a bag from the Guayaquil World Championships. She usually dawdles a bit, is slow to get in the water; she starts swimming near the end of her group with the slower people, and then, warming up, moves to the front to race against the fastest male swimmers in America. Then she stands out: a deep lode of natural ability and competitive drive. She is erratic in workouts: Her ambition comes and goes, seeming to run against a pain threshold. Her stroke is inelegant, almost spastic-looking as her head bobs with every stroke and jerks with every breath; but her arms are very long, and her hands swing out in front of her like gigantic ice-cream scoops, pulling her along. Tiffany began swimming at age eight, in Culver City, California, up north a little closer to Los Angeles, and had always shown a natural ability to move fast in the water. She came to the Mission Viejo team at age fourteen, and soon shot to the top of the national rankings, winning her first National Championship in the four-hundred free in 1981. Since then she had been the queen of distance freestyle, but there were always challengers: Kim Linehan from Sarasota; Marybeth Linzmeier, until recently a Mission swimmer; and now a fourteen-year-old from Miami named Michelle Richardson.

Sharing the lane with Cohen and usually swimming just behind her was her friend Florence Barker, also seventeen, who at five-three is noticeably small for a world-class swimmer. Barker is the third daughter from her family to swim at Mission; her older sister Vera was a few lanes over, with the medleyists. While Tiffany Cohen is quiet, Florence is talkative; while Tiffany seems shy, Florence is outgoing: laughing, joking, pulling little tricks, talking with everybody, at the center of the team's social life. Like Tiffany, Florence has an inelegant stroke, tailored less toward symmetrical beauty than toward survival of Schubert's workouts: Her arms swing over her head, one hand pushing forward low, almost through the water rather than over it. In races Florence regularly goes out in the first half ahead of the pack, trying finally to win; but she usually finishes third or fourth or fifth. Yet she is widely respected and cheered for—she is one of the few members of the team who has the real support of swimmers from other teams and their coaches. Florence is a worker, more consistent than Tiffany Cohen, probably one of the hardest-working swimmers on a hard-working team. Perhaps seeing Tiffany (and Channon Hermstad and Tami Bruce and her other friends) succeed so brilliantly while she is just a step behind keeps her hungry. Tiffany calls her "Flo," and on her pull buoy—the two plastic floats strung together used for supporting her legs during pulling drills—Tiffany has written in black ink, "FLO."

One more lane over, right next to the outside wall where Mark Schubert often stands, were the male distance swimmers. This is the so-called Animal Lane. Here were the hardest-working swimmers you could find, swimming the hardest workouts: Frank Iacono from France, John-Henry Escalas from Spain, Mike Davidson from New Zealand. These men and four or five others had come here to swim eighteen thousand to twenty thousand meters—twelve miles and more—every day against the most demanding time standards Mark Schubert could set. These were the swimmers who finished in the top eight at the European Championships, in the medals at Olympic Games—and who occasionally, for entertainment, would go over to Lake Mission Viejo, a huge artificial pond a full mile in length, and swim a morning practice consisting of an eight-lap race.

Now, in January 1983, leading the Animal Lane was Michael O'Brien; seventeen years old, six-six and 150 pounds, a long, strong, stringbean of a boy whose leaps-and-bounds improvement and unshakable belief in himself made him a strong if unknown contender for the 1984 Olympic Team; sometimes when Mark Schubert watched O'Brien in training, he remembered the fifteen-hundred-meter freestyle victor of the Montreal Games, another Mission distance star, and wondered if history could repeat itself and O'Brien might not become "the next Brian Goodell." O'Brien's height gives him an advantage in the free-style events where one swims the "crawl" stroke; his gigantic reach makes possible a relaxed, almost casual-looking pace, a rhythmic plop, plop, plop as his arms drop into the water and his huge, loose, flipperlike feet sweep steadily up and down as with each stroke he slides forward another six feet.

Born in Skokie, Illinois, O'Brien has lived most of his life twenty minutes up the freeway from Mission Viejo, in Costa Mesa. Around 1970, when he was five years old, Mike's parents took him with his two older sisters to the country club for swimming lessons and signed him up for the team as well. His sisters didn't especially like it, but he did, and continued swimming, becoming, over the next five or six years, one of the more successful age group swimmers in America. He regularly placed in the "top sixteen in the country" rankings; by the time he was twelve, he was very close to the national record for twelve-year-olds in the backstroke. His childhood years in the sport were easy and fun.

When he reached adolescence he lost some of his enthusiasm, became "sloppy," as he would later say. He wasn't sure he wanted to swim at all. He simply was not motivated. He started training seriously at age twelve, when Flip Darr, whose disbanded team had formed the nucleus of the early Mission Viejo Nadadores, returned to coaching and established a team called the Novaquatics in the town of Irvine, near Costa Mesa. When he was fourteen, during his freshman year in high school, he was forced to make a decision: Swimming requires a dedication perhaps not required of athletes in other sports—year-round training, strict attention to diet, consistent effort. For O'Brien, the issue came home one day in high-school PE class, during a basketball game: In the heat of play, he fell over on his left ankle, badly tearing the ligaments around it. It was a serious injury, one that could ruin a swimming career, one that would haunt him for years to come.

His parents took the opportunity to talk with their son. He had to decide, they told him, whether swimming would be important or not, whether he was willing to jeopardize his swimming for a little fun in a pickup basketball game. He had enjoyed some notable success as a youngster, but senior swimming—competition without the protection of age-bracketed events—demanded a much deeper commitment.

He decided they were right, and soon he left the Irvine Novaquatics to head south for the Mission Viejo Nadadores, where he could have world-class competition in workouts. He lifted weights, and he trained harder than ever before. For the first time in his life he swam "double workouts," two practices a day. To arrive at the first of these on time, he had to rise at four-thirty in the morning, since he lived so far from Mission Viejo. Years later, he would marvel that throughout his high-school years he rose at four-thirty every morning.

With every year at Mission Viejo, O'Brien swam noticeably faster—in the four-hundred-meter freestyle, an event that lasts about four minutes, as much as ten seconds faster every year. And every year he climbed higher in the national rankings. It isn't obvious to an outsider what makes O'Brien such a fierce competitor. He certainly doesn't appear ferocious. He has short hair and an open, friendly smile. He is generally very polite, a properly brought up young man, one might say, the sort of teenager of whom mothers are proud; and he also gets along well with most of his peers. In fact, pleasant and easygoing, he gets along "with pretty much everybody," in his own words. But he can surprise you with his drive in the water and with the seriousness of his intent. Having chosen a goal (which he does very carefully), he becomes singularly focused on achieving it. When he is in training, perhaps no one else at Mission Viejo watches his sleep so carefully and monitors his diet so closely as Mike O'Brien. Sometimes the other swimmers make fun of his conscientiousness; he is almost a goody-goody, they think, but they respect his dedication. In January 1983, Mike O'Brien was trying to win a National Championship, something he had never done; his best finish at Nationals was the previous summer, when he placed seventh in the fifteen hundred. But Schubert thought then that O'Brien was a winner, and O'Brien himself seemed never to doubt it. O'Brien knew that some of the best swimmers in the world, the best of all time, had swum there, over against the wall of the Marguerite pool, where he was now swimming; they had survived those workouts and prospered; and he, O'Brien, would survive these workouts, master them even; he, too, could win those big championships.

There were other Olympic hopefuls at Mission Viejo: Dave Louden in the middle-distance freestyles; Channon Hermstad in the four-hundred individual medley; Tami Bruce in the middle-distance freestyle races. And still more top swimmers would arrive in the summer—world record holders Ricardo Prado and Dara Torres among them.

Aside from those favorites, there were the scores of swimmers out there across the country, unknowns working toward the same goal. But in an Olympic year, they say, the unknowns have a pronounced tendency to join the ranks of the famous.

When Mark Schubert was coaching, few words were spoken. The workouts consisted entirely of "sets," groups of swims done on a given "interval"—that is, with a controlled amount of rest. A set may be "twenty-four hundreds on 1:05": That means the swimmers will do twenty-four swims of four lengths each (a hundred yards) and are allowed one minute and five seconds to complete each one before the next swim starts. Schubert would say little, other than giving them the set, but each word seemed to count. If someone did well, he'd say, perhaps once in a workout, "Nice job." If someone swam slower than he expected, he'd say, "That's not what I had in mind." While he was concerned with stroke techniques, he made only a few corrections he felt necessary. But with the physical suffering, the emotional stress of the upcoming Olympic Games, his brief comments carried tremendous weight.

Again, most spectators to the workouts couldn't feel that intensity, and most became bored within an hour. All they could see were forty teenagers swimming for miles and miles. That's all: nothing like a football scrimmage, with constant correction and encouragement and shouting, nothing like figure skating, with the continual appraisal of technique. Yet almost every day there were visiting coaches: One week there was one from Japan, another week one from Australia, coaches from the Midwest and from the East. Of them, Schubert says with a smile, they were "coming to Mecca to find out our secret." Usually after a few days, the visitors gradually grew bored as they began to think that this really wasn't so different, these guys really didn't know anything special (and, of course, they were right). Many of those coaches would go away thinking that Mission succeeded because of the money, the facilities, maybe the recruiting (which were all a part, but only a part, of the reason). Sometimes the visitors would leave, as one middle-aged man did, with little more than a picture of himself and Schubert, arms around shoulders, smiling for the Polaroid. After one visitor had been at Mission during that week in 1983, watching all the time, Schubert came over to him and asked, "Well, got us figured out yet?" The visitor said no, that it would take more than a week, maybe more than six months. Schubert chuckled and walked on. Schubert knew, and his visitor then suspected, that the "big secret" that all the visitors from around the world came looking for was—that there is no "big secret." There is only the will to swim for miles and miles, all the turns done correctly, all the strokes done legally, all the practices attended, all the weights lifted, and all the sprints pushed to the point of simple exhaustion, day after day for years and years. The magic, then—at least to that visitor—was disappearing from Mission Viejo; but the simple humanity of it was beginning to emerge.

Southern California is the land of the possible, or at least the belief of the possible. Despite its reputation for the easy life, of fun in the sun, California has a zeal for exercise that is puritanical. Supermarket aisles are filled with young women wearing nylon running shorts, tank tops, and sunglasses, with bodies very tan, with well-defined calf muscles; the state has 70 percent of the tri-athletes in America. Everyone, it seems, goes to the beach, and almost that many run for health.

So in Mission Viejo, working out is made easy. The whole culture is caught up in exercise—no one objects that you won't be well rounded or that the girls will get big shoulders. Working out is expected, and is expected to be pursued with a passion. California, hanging on the far edge of the continent, a land of opportunity, represents the last hope for staying young and fit and reaching all of your dreams; and here is where the better swimmers come to train, and to believe that it's still possible to be the best in the world.

4

The Human Contradictions

WHEN THE SUMMER BEGAN IN JUNE 1983, FLO BARKER AND
Tiffany Cohen, in one of the middle lanes; Mike O'Brien
(the tall distance swimmer) in the Animal Lane; and the
others (including Channon Hermstad, Tami Bruce, and
Dave Louden) were joined by a flock of collegians returning to train with the Nadadores. Ricardo Prado, world record holder in the four-hundred individual medley (and so
claimant at least to the unofficial title of "best all-around
swimmer in the world"), came from Southern Methodist
University in Dallas with his friend Rich Saeger; Dave
Barnes came from Harvard; Julie Williams came from
UCLA. Those schools, along with USC, Alabama, and
Arkansas, had strong ties with the Mission team, swapping
swimmers back and forth between the school year, when
they swam for their college teams, and the summer, when
they swam for Mission Viejo in U.S.S. competitions. There
were new swimmers, too—the most noticeable being Dara

Torres, the fastest woman in the world over a straight fifty meters. She was arguably the best sprinter alive, paradoxically joining a team known for endurance athletes. In the spring, over three hundred young swimmers had applied to join the Nadadores; Schubert had picked ten for his Senior National team, Torres being one of those. In this atmosphere, where long workouts are the norm, how do sprinters, with their talkative, flamboyant, high-spirited style ("When the going gets tough, the sprinters get out!") find a place?

Throughout that summer, there were the meets—the *Seventeen Magazine* Meet of Champions, the National Championships, the Pan American Games—all suffused with the promises of 1984, all taken as hints of what might happen in that next, and more important, year. Amid all the anxiety *(Will I make the Olympic team? Will there even be an Olympic team?)*, the swimmers looked for a sign, an omen of success: a finish that would be high enough, an improvement that could be extrapolated.

Flo Barker and Tiffany Cohen and their friends called him Ricky—"Reeky" was how they said it. His name was Ricardo Prado, and in some ways he typified many of the men returning from college that summer. With his dark, Latin good looks, the girls thought he was very cute. He was short, maybe five-six, the smallest man on a team of seventy swimmers, with curly brown hair and a squarish face and a shy grin. The youngest of five children, he grew up in São Paulo, Brazil. Swimming since the age of five, he was watched by coaches there, who told his parents that Ricardo was talented, that in Brazil he was not getting the kind of training that he needed to do his best. Prado read *Swimming World* magazine and had heard of Mission Viejo, of Jesse Vassallo, the world record holder in the IM (individual medley), of Brian Goodell and Casey Converse, had heard of the Animal Lane and those incredible workouts. So when he was thirteen he wrote a letter—his mother translated it, since Ricardo didn't know English—to Mark Schubert and asked permission to come to California and swim for the Mission Viejo Nadadores. Schubert wrote back, *Wait a while, you're only thirteen; you can come in two years.* So Prado waited; and in two years he came up to live with a family in Mission Viejo. He entered Mission Viejo High as a junior.

For all of that year and all of the next he swam the Animal Lane workouts, five and six hours a day. (He also learned English—by 1983 he spoke it quite well.) He didn't really like the training, he had never liked training, but he had to do it. He was not tall enough, not fast enough, to swim the sprints, so he had to go the distances: the two-hundred fly, the two-hundred back, the four-hundred individual medley. Often when he swam, he was so bored that he would sing songs to make the time pass. After two years of training at Mission Viejo, in the summer of 1982, at age seventeen, he represented Brazil at the World Championships in Guayaquil, Ecuador. There he broke the world record in the four-hundred IM.

In a way, the world record hurt him: He was left without any big goals in swimming. Actually, the questioning had started maybe six months earlier; he had begun to doubt what he was doing: Was it all worth it, living in a pool for six hours a day? This wasn't the way he wanted to live. He had thought, *Maybe the world record will get me going;* he had thought, *Maybe breaking the record, winning the World Championships, will make a big change and be exciting.* But it wasn't that great, it didn't really change anything at all. He was good at swimming, very good, and he needed the sport. If he quit there would be no college scholarship anymore, no ten thousand dollars each year to go to SMU and swim. But during the summer of 1983 Ricardo Prado just wasn't into swimming anymore. He hated the training and he didn't like the way Schubert treated some of the people on the team, sort of like they were little children. It bothered him, he said, sometimes it almost made him sick seeing some guy doing push-ups for having a bad turn. *What is this*, he thought, *the army?* Schubert treated Prado himself decently, better than before he had entered college, but the distance people and the medleyists, it seemed to Prado, had life worse than the sprinters; they had to work out with Schubert all the time, and Mark was very tough. Scott MacFarland ran the sprinters' practices, and he was a little looser in workouts, a little more fun. Prado was tired of it all—the workouts, the pressure, Schubert—but he had to keep swimming because he was so good. With only one year to go until the Olympics it would be stupid to quit.

Prado's dissatisfaction was extreme, but in milder forms such complaints were widespread among the men returning from college. They had seen life beyond the swimming pool, and they liked it. The college coaches weren't as dictatorial as the club coaches; college athletes were older and spent more time on their own in classes, at parties, in the dorm, with friends, and gave less of their lives grinding out laps in the pool. Even the most serious college teams didn't do the kind of workouts that the club teams, filled with high schoolers, did. The college teams raced shorter distances, and they had meets more often, usually every week. Their swimmers were more specialized as well. So while many of the college swimmers loved the sport and appreciated the program at Mission for the opportunities it offered, their acceptance of Mark Schubert and his authoritarian style of coaching was not uncritical.

They brought this new attitude with them to Mission in the summertime, and Schubert saw it—the college men were a little more casual, more lackadaisical perhaps, even a touch lazy sometimes—and it bothered him, it violated his sense of control. Every day at practice there were little incidents, little discipline problems. One day, two men walked in late. Schubert said, "Sorry, fellas, once or twice is okay, but it's gotten to the point where you come on time or you don't come at all." He told them just to go home. The next day, another did an illegal (one-hand) finish at the end of a breaststroke swim; Schubert told him to get out and do fifty push-ups. The next day Schubert pulled still another aside near the end of practice and said to him, "Going to the beach is fine, but if you want to be on this team, you have to come to practice." He paused and then pointed to the swimmers in the water. "You see these guys? They want to be national champions, and as a team we want to be national champions. If you want to be one, you can train with us. If you don't, you can train somewhere else. You understand me?" The boy, looking down, nodded. "Now, I don't hold a grudge," Schubert said, "but I don't want to talk about this again. Okay?"

But he needed the college men; they were the fastest swimmers. And they needed Schubert's program, the competition, the unmatched facilities, the pool time. So the swimmers and the coaches lived with each other, sometimes a little uneasily.

For the women, things were different. The key fact was physical: Females mature earlier than males. This means that at age thirteen or fourteen, some girls are going to the National or World championships or even to the Olympics. Sometimes at age fourteen (Sippy Woodhead in 1979) or at fifteen (Shane Gould in 1972) a girl can break a world record, especially in one of the distance events, where sheer size and muscle bulk matter less than endurance and hard work; at that age the female body is still slim enough to offer little resistance to the water. So some girls become nationally known when they are still children, under the strict control of their parents and their coaches, when the coach is more of a father figure than a teacher or colleague. Children at this age swim with their parents' support and usually strong encouragement; they are dependent.

Schubert built his team with younger girls who swam year-round with him (not leaving for college like the top-rank older men). They could do those long-distance workouts, physically, perhaps more easily than the boys: Girls seem to have better endurance; perhaps because of their greater body fat they could swim the longer distances without muscles breaking down. In general, the really high-mileage programs seem to be built around women. Coach Richard Shoulberg of Germantown Academy, giving his swimmers up to thirty thousand meters in a day, has a team that produces mostly great girls; Paul Bergen, who developed Tracy Caulkins, coaches mostly girls; Mark Schubert has built a program around the girls. (In fairness, all of these coaches have top male swimmers, too.) The world record for the English Channel crossing has been held by women. As the distances grow longer, the women, it seems, catch up with the men.

But beginning around age fifteen and certainly by sixteen or seventeen, the fat difference really starts to show. The weight gain for women comes in the hips and thighs and breasts, the muscles become less defined, and a body that once looked like a boy's now looks like a woman's, and it won't move quite as quickly. For the women who continue swimming, and fight against the slowdown that comes, weight can become an obsession. Male coaches often don't seem to understand the fluctuations of the menstrual cycle, how weight can change so much in a few days; a once-a-week weigh-in doesn't tell the story. Sometimes the women fall into the familiar symptoms of bulimia, purging; some take laxatives or black beauties; others the less dangerous path of running miles a day, carefully watching their food intake. Schubert has the Mission swimmers take a body fat test once a month, and sometimes some of the women try to cheat a little, pushing themselves up on the sides of the water submersion tank, just a little, afraid of what the computations might show: *I'm fat.*

Around them they see the boys swimming faster, getting sleeker and longer and harder, more powerful rather than less, improving by leaps just as the girls slow down. There are many great female swimmers at twelve, thirteen, fourteen years old, but by nineteen many have left the sport, realizing that the great highs may be past and that there are things in life beyond swimming. Still, by 1987, the growth of athletic scholarships and more public support for women in sports had pushed up the median age of women on the U.S. National team to nineteen.

With the move to college, for those who remain, things change dramatically. For the women, college means they are, for the first time, really independent of parents and coaches—and the jolt seems bigger for girls than for boys, who were less protected at earlier ages, less controlled and constrained by parents, less closely chaperoned by coaches. Girls discover, as 1976 Olympic gold medalist Wendy Boglioli puts it, "There's fun things . . . I could be doing. 'Oh, God, I can go out on a *date* this weekend'. . . . And a lot of them . . . can't really handle it, too many things going on in my life, it's just easier to quit."

Yet many coaches, at the college level, say there is no difference between women and men. Maybe, for the ones who stay, there isn't: Maybe the women who decide to swim in college are doing it more for themselves than for their parents—the same as the men. But it seems, at almost every level, that girls swim with the support of their parents, while boys often swim in defiance of their parents. For girls, the sport is one of childhood, done when one is young; for boys—and this is supported by their physical development as well—the sport is one of young adulthood, if anything a sign of moving away from the arbitrary authority of others. Girls seem often to change coaches after going away to college, even if they continue swimming. College coaches treat them like adults, not, as Wendy Boglioli puts it, "like little neuters."

What doesn't change for the girls, or later, the women, is that they care how the coach treats them, in a more personal way than do the boys and men. Many males in swimming don't like their coach, but for most that is a nearly irrelevant fact to their swimming; but the females either love or hate their coach, and which it is makes all the difference.

Here were mixed, day in and day out, two vastly different groups, socially and physically speaking, there together because, in practices at least and over longer distances, they swam at close to the same speed: fifteen-, sixteen-, seventeen-year-old girls and twenty-two-, twenty-three-year-old men; both groups in superb physical condition (and obviously so), in a setting of high emotional intensity, near-constant pain, tremendous pressure, wearing revealing costumes, the excitement of it, the admitted eroticism of it ("Why are swimmers so horny?" one swimmer asked one day)—the dynamics are incredible. The coaches know this. Schubert used to forbid dating among team members, and even now he discourages it; at meets the boys and the girls from Mission are housed on separate floors in the hotels. But despite his close control over their activities, despite the sometimes all-consuming focus on athletic training and competition, here is one of the few sports in which males and females actively train and travel together, and the opportunities for an engaging social life are tremendous.

Swimming is a sport of adolescence, of children becoming adults. Participation in the sport is made possible only by parental support. Swimming is an amateur sport, so only those people with lots of free time—that is, children—can participate. So when Shirley Babashoff in the mid-1970s came to practice at Marguerite all those mornings, her mother drove her. Parents pay plane fares and entry fees and pay for suits and warm-up suits and caps and goggles. For a national-level competitor the whole business can easily cost over five thousand dollars a year. God only knows how many potentially great swimmers never made it because their parents didn't have that kind of money to throw into leisure activity that would never bring back any financial returns (beyond, maybe, a college scholarship, if the kid was really good). Once the parents are making it all possible, paying the bills and driving to all those practices twice a day all year long and going to meets every other weekend, they start wanting Junior to do a little better ("Your mother and I are sacrificing a lot for this; you'd better get your act together"); and they start thinking about those college scholarships. Pretty soon the whole thing is really a family enterprise, where full sets of brothers and sisters are all swimming, Dad is head of the Booster Club, and Mom is the team secretary (in the typical situation), and the kids find that they can't get out even if they want to. That is, for the kids, the big danger.

"The kids" is what they are called, too. Coaches talk about "the kids," and parents and officials do, too. "The kids are what this is all about," they say, but the adults still own the pools, organize and officiate the meets, and coach the teams . Adults decide who is eligible and who is not, where you can swim and how much it will cost. Swimming may be a sport for children, but it is run by adults; and only in the past few years, with a few commercial opportunities creeping in, do older athletes—twenty-three, twenty-four years old—stay in the sport and have some influence over the rules, the chaperone policies, the curfews, and so on. Among the older athletes—traditionally the boys, who physically peak later, and who had, all along, the college swimming opportunities—the resistance to that adult authority is greater, producing the wild carryings-on of the college men's teams and leading to the sort of difficulties Mark Schubert faced with the college swimmers who came back to Mission in the summer of 1983.

The young swimmers like the independence of the sport. For the fact is, one of the great attractions of swimming to its devotees is that the results are objective, and nobody else can claim the success. Many swimmers say that in lives dominated by other people—parents, teachers, coaches—in the pool, competing against others, what they do is their own, and how well they do it is absolute. If the coach hates you, he still can't make you swim slow; if you're ugly, the judges can't deduct points. Being unattractive or unpopular won't reduce your score, as it often seems to in ice skating or diving. Reputation doesn't count. Every day in practice, and in every meet, you know exactly how well you are doing. There is a blunt honesty in the sport. "In swimming," says Dick Shoulberg, a national-level coach, "a 1:09 is a 1:09, and no amount of bullshit can make it a 1:06."

It seems, too, that the better the teams, the more the parents are kept out of the swimming itself and directed into support activities like fundraising. The great teams like Mission Viejo often either board swimmers from out of town (housing them with local team members), or are actually affiliated with such boarding schools as Germantown or Mercersburg or Pine Crest, or such colleges as the Universities of Florida or Texas. There are exceptions—the Cincinnati Pepsi Marlins, or the Nashville Aquatic Club—but the trend is to separate the athletes from their parents, and often it seems like that's what the athletes, "the kids," want. "Swimming was a chance," says one Olympian, "to get out of the house and away from my parents for four hours a day. They didn't want me to do it—my dad thought swimming was a sissy sport."

So the variety within the Mission Viejo team in the summer of 1983 was now evident: the children and the adults; the men and the women; and, finally, a new distinction, rare on this team of distance swimmers, the sprinters, who were really a different breed. One swimmer in particular exemplified the sprinter's style and abilities, and the headaches sprinters could give coaches and the resentments they could generate among the others, like Prado, who had to do the long workouts. Her talent was incredible. Her name was Dara Torres.

Dara Torres is the stereotypical sprinter. Tall, good-looking, with stylishly cut short brown hair and perfect teeth, she is talkative and outgoing, striking up conversations with anybody who comes by, moving from one person to the next. At the *Seventeen Magazine* Meet of Champions that summer at Mission Viejo she wore a Sony Walkman everywhere; it was a kind of trademark. She and her friends would swap tapes: Van Halen, heavy metal of all kinds; she also liked the *Chariots of Fire* theme, an inspirational piece for her. She chews anything in reach: fingers, towels, goggle straps, gum. She is a little jumpy but very personable, loves having her picture taken and making funny faces for photographers, who love her for loving them and for being so attractive.

She was born wealthy. Her mother, Marylu, was a model; her father, Ed Torres—her parents divorced when Dara was eight—is in real estate, among other things; in 1983 he was the owner of the Aladdin Hotel in Las Vegas. Her stepfather, Ed Kauder, is a professional tennis player. The family—Dara, her four older brothers, a younger sister, and Marylu and Ed Kauder—lives in a mansion in Beverly Hills with nine bedrooms and 10½ baths. Dara Torres drives around town in a 1979 Mercedes 300 TD station wagon. Besides having money, she is blessed with height— five-ten—and "70 percent fast twitch" muscle fiber. This means that she can contract her muscles more quickly than most people, even noticeably faster than the average Mission Viejo swimmer. The reports are that she can tolerate a concentration of eighteen millimoles of lactic acid in her blood, a physiologically measurable tolerance of pain that is stunningly high. In other words, she can swim very hard, pushing her muscles past the point where most people's muscles would simply collapse. She is gifted in other sports and has played football and baseball, often being the first chosen in coed games. She was usually team captain in sports at school.

Dara Torres began swimming at the age of nine, and at ten she began swimming at a YMCA in Beverly Hills, where her coach was Karen Moe Thornton, an Olympian from 1972. In two years Torres made the YMCA Nationals, a good but not great meet, and there she saw how serious some people were. She came back from that meet and went over to Culver City, to a coach she had known when she was a little younger. With that coach, Terry Palma, she made the U.S.S. Nationals. In the spring of 1982, when she was fourteen years old, she went to Gainesville for the Nationals, swimming the fifty free (she had never been able to go much farther than a fifty, the shortest event; she had never liked working hard, had never really done much with all that speed beyond going the sprints). Here she was, this young unknown, climbing up on the starting blocks to swim the fifty free against Jill Sterkel, the dominant woman sprinter in America—unbeaten over the past several years in this event.

The day before, Torres had gone to a movie theater, seen *Chariots of Fire,* and been inspired by it. In the preliminaries she had qualified second, and now in the finals was in the lane next to Sterkel; the race would match an older woman, a gold medalist from the 1976 Olympics, against a fourteen-year-old nobody from Culver City, California.

One year later, Torres remembered:

I wasn't that big [a name], and it was really neat . . . and I'm in lane five all the way, nervous and everything. I'm getting

all ready and everything, and so [the guns fires and] I take off
. . . and I finish, hit the wall, and the old lady, this timer,
bends over and says, "You did it." And I turned around and
looked at my time, and I was cheering, and I looked at my
coach and he comes over, gives me a kiss, people were clap-
ping, and I was just amazed. They pulled me out of the water,
the TV cameras are on me and they're doing interviews and
everything and I was like so nervous, even after the race . . .
my coach comes over and says, "Hey, you just made your
first U.S.A. trip!," there was a trip after that meet, and I was
just on cloud nine.

And standing up there getting the gold medal it was just
the neatest experience, and that night I couldn't go to
sleep. . . .

Years later she would laugh at herself with some embar-
rassment; she had been so young, and success had been so
easy. There were to be other highs after that. In the spring
of 1983, at a meet in Holland, Torres set a new unofficial
world record in the fifty-meter freestyle—there was no officially recognized event at that distance internationally,
but Torres had the "best time" at the distance.

She knew there would be no fifty at the Olympics; there
was only the hundred. She had never done the hard work,
the endurance work, it would take to make the Olympic
team in the hundred. So she thought about going to Fort
Lauderdale, Florida, to train with Jack Nelson, a former
Olympic coach, but that was too far from her family. So she
talked with Mark Schubert and decided that at Mission she
would have the competition and would get the kind of distance training she needed but had never really done. She
left her old coach, Terry Palma, at Culver City—now Tan-
dem Swim Club—and moved down to Mission to live with
Mike and Flor Stutzman, who had a ten-year-old on the
Mission team. "I just came here," she said, "to get more
guts." With a tough coach and an endurance program she
would have to work harder—although at Mission the repu-

tation continued, that Dara didn't do the practices very seriously, that she climbed out when things got too tough, pulling on the lane lines, cheating on sets, and the like. She knew this about herself; she was at Mission, in fact, because she knew this, and knew that there, more than anywhere else, she couldn't really get away with it. Schubert knew he had to push her (she wanted a tough coach standing over her), but he knew, too, that a sprinter, with natural speed like hers, could get burned out, and he didn't want to overtrain her; that was a real danger. He told *Sports Illustrated*, "We have to judge how much endurance stuff we can do without getting her overtired. With distance kids, we want them to be tired. But with Dara, we don't want to ever enter the Valley of Fatigue. That's when training gets negative for her."

That was difficult for Schubert. He spent time instilling in his athletes the idea that hard work was a real virtue, was the measure of worth, of prestige. The Animal Lane was a symbol of this sentiment. Swimmers at Mission took pride in doing the hardest workouts, the longest sets. Here was a swimmer—the fastest in the world, no less—who didn't like to work. She could do maybe nine thousand meters a day, but not eighteen thousand. And Schubert seemed to treat her very well, not quite sure what to do. He had never been thought of as a sprint coach before, but now "I guess I have to learn to coach sprinters. I've got the best one in the world." His job was to give Torres endurance without damaging her incredible speed; her job (and Schubert regularly talks about training and competing in those terms, saying, for instance, "We have a job to do at this meet," or "Good job" after a swim, very solid and businesslike) was to swim the hundred without dying over the last thirty meters. She arrived at Mission in June 1983, one of the ten new swimmers and probably the most likely of them to make the 1984 Olympic Team, but it wouldn't be easy. Winning was not the only thing at Mission, but working toward winning, it seemed, was. Schubert appreciates physical courage; and his assistant, Scott MacFarland, could tell you in detail, with vivid adjectives and nouns, who worked hard and who didn't. What counted at Mission, often, was who did the hard training, and Dara Torres seemed to have some trouble with that.

Between just the two of them, Dara Torres and Ricardo Prado represented the broad diversity of swimmers on the Mission Viejo team, and in world-class swimming as a whole. Torres was young, living near home, swimming for a strong coach—the kind she needed and wanted—and female. She was a sprinter, blessed with natural speed that in some ways required that she work less than her teammates. For her, swimming was a leisure activity that brought excitement and a little fame.

Prado's story was clearly quite different. He had begged to join the team, and he had been turned down the first time. He left home when quite young, and he came to a foreign country where he didn't even know the language, just to swim. He was a hero back in Brazil, always under pressure to bring some glory to a country that rarely won swimming events. He was older now, a college man, who needed the scholarship money swimming brought to support himself. His success had come from long, hard work and would continue only as long as the work continued; he had made a deep commitment to swimming. Far from seeing Mark Schubert as any kind of revered father figure, Prado saw him merely as someone who gave him the training that made his own hard-won success possible.

5

The Pan American Games

MIKE O'BRIEN, THE TALL, THIN DISTANCE SWIMMER, DIDN'T train very well during that summer. He knew it, and Schubert knew it. Neither was expecting any great swims from O'Brien at the National Championships held in Clovis, California, in early August. But the Clovis meet would be where the U.S. team to the Pan American Games would be chosen, and the Pan Ams would be a kind of preview of the Olympics. That excited O'Brien. So he pointed for the Clovis meet just to get to the Pans Ams. As it happened, his four hundred was not very good, and so he was left, by the end of the meet, with only one chance to make the team, in the fifteen-hundred free.

All heats save the final, fastest were swum in the morning session of the meet. In one of the heats Dave Sims from Stanford swam the fifteen hundred in fifteen minutes, twenty-four and fourteen one-hundredths of a second (15:24.14)—faster than O'Brien's best by five seconds. So

O'Brien knew before his race that evening that to make the top two—to make the Pan Am team—he would have to go faster than Sims' time and do no worse than second in this final heat as well.

Before the race, O'Brien talked with Rafael Escalas, who would be holding the lap cards telling how many lengths had been swum in the race. Escalas was supposed to put the cards into the water at the end of the lane as O'Brien came into the wall to remind him where he was. In addition, O'Brien asked Escalas to hold one or more fingers underwater against the cards to show how many seconds under the 15:30 pace O'Brien was swimming. O'Brien knew that he needed to see all five fingers in order to be even with Sims' time from the morning, to have a chance to make the Pan Am team.

He started fast, jumped out to a four-second—four-finger—lead, and for most of the thirty laps in the race, as he came up to each turn at the far end, he saw four of Escalas' fingers. Jeff Kostoff, swimming in the next lane, was way out ahead by the end, winning by six seconds. With only one lap left—fifty meters, one length—there were still only four fingers. Mark Schubert, standing on the deck watching, saw O'Brien go wild, sprinting like he never had before. He touched that last wall at 15:24.00. He had beaten Sims by fourteen one-hundredths of a second and made the Pan Am team. Schubert was impressed by the finish. It was the most aggressive race he had ever seen O'Brien swim, chasing down Sims' splits that way, and he told O'Brien afterward that he should be that aggressive during the body of the race, during all those other twenty-nine laps. O'Brien decided to try that strategy at the Pan Ams.

The Pan American trip would be O'Brien's first time representing the United States on an international team. He didn't know more than five or six other swimmers on the team, being a newcomer to world-class swimming, and at seventeen would be one of the youngest males there. The team went to Fort Lauderdale for a training camp at the Swimming Hall of Fame pool just two blocks from the Strip and Fort Lauderdale Beach. One day at the hotel where the team was staying, in Hollywood just south of Fort Lauderdale, all the swimmers were taken into a huge room filled with piles and piles of Levi's Official Pan Am Games sweats, jeans, shirts, and parade outfits; there were leather shoes, sandals, three pieces of luggage to hold all the clothes, jogging pants, and rainsuits; O'Brien had never seen such equipment, lots and lots of it, all given the swimmers free, mostly from Levi's (Arena gave swimsuits, and other companies donated other things). He was excited by the attention and the free equipment that said "U.S.A.," by meeting the other swimmers and training with them; it was his *first national team*, and it was all very fresh and exciting for him.

The Pan Am Games were held in Caracas, Venezuela, and the setting put a damper on some of the excitement: The pool was beautiful, and the crowds were very enthusiastic, very friendly, but the Pan Am village itself was scattered among some small, isolated towns 1½ or two hours from the pool. Some of the buildings were unfinished. O'Brien came away with the impression of dirt and dust, of fresh cement dormitories with "showers" that were just a hole in the wall with a drain. In the women's dorm the toilets and sewers overflowed, and so the women had to move into the men's building. There were no shelves on the walls, so some of the swimmers pulled the mattresses off onto the floor and used the bare bedsprings for shelves. It was the first time O'Brien had been to a Third World nation, and it was a culture shock for him. For those more experienced—for instance, Head Coach Don Gambril, who was to be the head Olympic coach in 1984—it was certainly no worse than many other countries and probably better than Mexico City during the 1968 Olympics, which had been terrible: the food, the water, the infections, the altitude, the traffic, everything.

If the housing in Caracas was bad, the transportation was worse, more congested even than in Los Angeles, with unbelievable traffic jams, miles and miles of four-lane traffic, bumper-to-bumper automobiles. The team buses would pick up the swimmers on time, at eight in the morning, and then, wedging themselves into the stream of cars, would struggle through downtown Caracas, with motorcycle escorts racing ahead. On a good day the twenty-five miles to the pool took forty minutes; on a bad day (and Gambril timed it) it took one hour and fifty-two minutes.

Fortunately, few of the swimmers came down with the usual gastrointestinal problems. The American team staff had prepared detailed information for the swimmers on what to avoid eating and drinking and how to avoid various local infections. Jill Sterkel, the twenty-three-year-old veteran of the 1976 Olympics, had some problems with stomach cramps on the last day of the meet, and Dara Torres went home early feeling sick, but it wasn't a major problem for the team.

O'Brien swam the four-hundred individual medley, an event he often competed in for the break it gave him from freestyle. He knew he couldn't win against Ricardo Prado, his Mission Viejo teammate who was there swimming for his home country, Brazil. He swam to win a medal, and he did, taking third.

But the fifteen hundred was O'Brien's race, and he wanted to win it. Usually he was conservative, planning his race carefully, knowing all the way how fast he was going. But this time he decided just to go out, take the lead from the start, and try to hang on. It was a totally different strategy from his usual come-from-behind tactic.

For the first half of the race, it worked. He was leading at eight hundred meters, and then he saw Jeff Kostoff creeping up, little by little. At a thousand meters Kostoff was even, and Kostoff, O'Brien knew, was the competition; he was more experienced, the leading American distance swimmer. For the next five or six laps—250 to three hundred meters—they fought back and forth, but now Kostoff had the initiative and was fresher, O'Brien having spent himself on gaining the early lead. With two hundred meters—four laps—to go, O'Brien came into the wall, flipped, and tried to see where Kostoff was. In that moment the goggle on O'Brien's left eye leaked a little and filled with water, blinding him on the side toward Kostoff. O'Brien's concentration broke, and he panicked for a moment. He had been caught concentrating too much on the other swimmer, and, when for a moment he lost sight of him, everything seemed to fall apart. Kostoff left him, and then the others started going by. O'Brien finished in fourth place.

It was a new experience for him, and a bad one. Always before he had had the great training to fall back on. In fact, O'Brien had always swum "negative splits," going faster in the second half of the race. Each successive part of the race ("split") took less time than the preceding part (hence "negative"). His strong point was finishing fast, until now. If his new strategy of starting fast was to work, he had to build up, over the long months ahead, the endurance to hold a faster pace longer. He knew that, and so he planned to do it. O'Brien never seemed deeply bothered by bad swims; he always just took them as one more lesson learned, an opportunity to discover—and then overcome—his weaknesses.

For Dara Torres, the Clovis Nationals were to be the first test of her training at Mission Viejo; she would find out if the heavy-distance workouts would in fact help her sustain that blinding speed over a distance of a hundred meters instead of only the flat-sprint fifty. Before, she had always "died" on the second fifty; but now, to make the Pan Am team (as to make the Olympic Team in 1984), she would have to place in the top four in the hundred free; there would be four swimmers in the four-by-hundred relay, two in the individual hundred free.

She was seeded twenty-fifth when the meet began; she needed to place fourth. In the preliminary heats in the morning she swam beautifully, making the finals and qualifying first. She hadn't died during the second lap. Schubert chuckled a bit after that race, knowing that she had come to Mission to gain that ability to hang on and that her faith had been justified. He had trained a great sprinter to last a hundred meters, and he had done it without destroying her speed. Torres spent the afternoon in her hotel room, pacing back and forth, and her palms, it seemed to her, were dripping sweat. She went to Schubert's room and asked for help, and he talked to her, calming her down a little, but she was still nervous. She had proven in the morning prelims that she could go out hard and not die; but that night the crowds were there, and the TV cameras, and she was very scared. The race started; she went out well in the first fifty, turned, and blasted off the wall, sprinting all out rather than building to a finish, and near the end . . . she died. Three girls passed her, and she finished fourth. That was good enough to make the relay, but not the individual hundred. Nevertheless, she had made the Pan Am team.

There was a fifty free, too, her best event, at Nationals, even though there wouldn't be one on the Pan Ams. A year before, Torres had set a world's best record in the fifty, and that was something she was proud of. She knew that just before Nationals someone had broken it, but she didn't know the girl's name (it was Anne-Marie Verstappen of the Netherlands). Torres wanted the record back. During the morning prelims, it was hot outside. She felt a little drained and wasn't in a lane next to either of the two other fastest girls, Jill Sterkel and Carrie Steinseifer. But she swam well anyway, recording a 25.72, only three one-hun-dredths of a second off her old record, the one that Ver-stappen had just broken.

In the finals that evening, she was nervous again, but not like in the hundred. When the starter said, "Take your marks," she dropped into her starting position, a "track start" with one foot behind the other. Unusual in swim-ming, it allowed her to catapult forward off the blocks. The starter hesitated, Torres started to come forward a bit early, and fearing a false start and disqualification, she pulled herself back. The videotape replays clearly show that mo-ment as she rocked back on her heels and stopped almost dead, helpless, at the exact moment the starter sounded the horn to start the shortest sprint event there is in swimming; she was caught leaning backward, away from the pool, moving in precisely the wrong direction. The rest of the field, Steinseifer and Sterkel and the others, took off. Then Torres pulled hard on the front of the blocks, rolled for-ward, and dove in after them.

She surged forward in the greatest display of raw speed ever exhibited by a female swimmer. Her tremendous strength, her beautiful stroke technique, her ability to focus all her energy on a single point—the far end of the pool— came together flawlessly. By the halfway mark, twenty-five meters down the pool, she had caught the field; by the end of the race she led the others by a body length. Her time was 25.62, a new world's best time. She wondered a bit afterward what the time would have been if her start had been better. But, she thought, it was still an okay swim. She hoped to do well at Pan Ams.

For Torres, as for O'Brien, the trip down to Caracas for the Pan Ams was the first visit to Latin America, and in the week before the swimming competition opened, after the opening ceremonies (which made her think, *This is a little like the Olympics, maybe this is what the Olympics will be like*), Torres and some of the other swimmers walked around town. They marveled at how cheap everything was; in the shops several of them bought Sony Walkmans (they cost only about forty dollars), and Dara bought one for her brother, since she herself already owned one, her constant companion at swimming meets.

The freestyle relay was her only event. The American team had a chance at breaking the world record if every swimmer could make a :55. Torres was scheduled to swim the lead-off leg, but the pressure of setting the pace for the others scared her. She approached Don Gambril and asked if he might move her. He knew she was nervous. That wasn't unusual; the lead-off leg was a tough one, so he let Dara swim second, after the veteran Jill Sterkel, who swam the lead-off leg. Torres swam the fastest leg on the relay (56:44), which had been her goal, but they didn't get the world record. In fact, they didn't even come close.

Ricardo Prado was the only male swimmer not from the United States to win a gold medal in the 1983 Pan Am swimming competition, that coming in the four-hundred-meter individual medley. In Brazil, after the Pan Ams, they wondered if their countryman Prado would also win a gold medal in Los Angeles (the next year, even *Swimming World* would wonder, running a cover story: "Ricardo Prado: Can He Return Brazil to the Gold Standard?"). Now that the summer was over, he would return to SMU in Dallas, where the swimming was more fun, a little easier perhaps.

The Pan Ams had been Mike O'Brien's first international meet and Dara Torres' second. Both of them were still high schoolers, relatively inexperienced, and both had felt the pressure. But they still had the luxury to make mistakes, for the Olympics were a year away, and Dara Torres and Mike O'Brien were on their way up, with visions of greater things ahead.

The U.S. swimming team won twenty-five of twenty-nine gold medals at the 1983 Pan American Games. By the meet's end, American men held world records in all four strokes. For the women, Caracas was a near sweep as well, as they took twelve of fourteen events. The men now looked forward to a good showing at Los Angeles, but the women knew, and their coaches knew, that the East Germans would probably prevent that. At the European Championships, which Mark Schubert had attended in Rome, Italy, that summer, the East German women took *first and second in every event*. Some coaches realized that the American women would in all likelihood be trounced at the Olympics, and the public would see that as a failure of U.S. swimming programs. The tremendous depth of U.S. swimming wouldn't be visible, only the lack of gold medalists. Mary T. Meagher could win the butterfly races, and Tracy Caulkins might win the four-hundred IM; but other than that, the American women had a long, long way to go.

6

Friends and Rivals

AT THOSE SAME PAN AMERICAN GAMES, ROWDY GAINES—
the world record holder in the hundred-meter freestyle—
almost retired from swimming. On the opening night of the
competition, in the two-hundred free, one of his best
events, in which he had once held the world record, he
finished third. He was devastated. "I went back to my room
and cried for hours. I had swum my last race. That was it,"
he told *Swimming World*. Gaines, though, was a team
leader, and his loss would be a loss for the entire U.S.
team. Some of the veterans—Jill Sterkel, Sippy Woodhead,
Rick Carey—talked with Gaines and tried to bolster his
confidence. Don Gambril, the Americans' head coach,
talked with him for three hours one afternoon, telling him
not to worry. *You don't need a great two hundred*, he told
him, *to have a great Olympics. You don't have to be Mark
Spitz; no one has to win seven gold medals.* Ever since
Munich, Olympic swimmers had been measured by that

nearly impossible standard of seven gold medals. Gambril told Gaines, as he told others, *Winning just one gold medal is a great accomplishment, one to cherish for the rest of your life. You don't necessarily have to get five.* If Gaines swam the hundred free in Los Angeles, then the four-by-hundred free relay, then the freestyle anchor leg on the four-by-hundred medley relay, that would be three medals right there, an accomplishment anyone could be proud of. Rowdy Gaines felt better for having Gambril's support and he came back later in the Pan Ams and won the hundred free. Then the American medley relay team, with the four world record holders in the individual strokes—Rick Carey, Steve Lundquist, Matt Gribble, and Gaines—won the relay and set a new world record. It seemed then that Rowdy Gaines was back in swimming, for a while at least.

Actually, Gaines had retired several times and was earning a dubious reputation as a perpetual "comeback" swimmer. He had first retired after his world-record hundred-meter freestyle swim, in 1981. But his time in that event (49.36) had in fact barely beaten the previous world record (49.44) held by South African Jonty Skinner, and Gaines was not satisfied that his record would stand long. He also worried sometimes that the record swim was not quite legitimate, as it was set in a time trial at the Texas Swim Center in Austin, where the conditions were perfect, with no one else in the pool and so fewer waves. Breaking a world record in meet competition with pressure and the turbulence was another matter. So he wanted to continue swimming. On the other hand, the '84 Games were at that point several years away, and he didn't want to be, as he told *Swimming World,* "one of those guys who hangs on and on, telling himself that he can still be competitive when he knows good and well he can't. . . ." So he stopped swimming that spring and went back to his mother's home in Winter Haven, Florida, where he played some billiards with friends, drank some beer, and eventually got bored.

His retirement lasted through the summer. By October 1981 he was back in the water, training. The six-month layoff had hurt him, and for the fall and winter he played catch-up, just trying to get through the workouts. But catch up he did, and he won Nationals in April 1982 in the hundred and two-hundred freestyles. He was already twenty-two years old. By the time of the 1984 Olympics, Ambrose "Rowdy" Gaines IV would be twenty-four, far older than most American swimmers.

He grew up in central Florida, where his mother was a water skier in the world-famous Cypress Gardens extravaganza. Gaines learned how to swim at an early age, paddling around in Lake Eloise near his home. In the summers of his eighth and ninth years he swam on a local country club team. After that, swimming was no more than a recreation for him. He loved other sports—baseball, basketball, football, tennis—and while he was growing up he played all of them, although never in very competitive situations.

By high school, though, he was more ambitious. He needed something to do, a direction to his life, and he realized that if he didn't find one he could easily wind up pumping gas at the local service station. Besides, his parents would not be able to send him to college unless he could help; and he knew that there were sports scholarships. He was too small for football, only five-eight or five-nine and weighing 130 pounds; too short for basketball; and at tennis and golf, which he enjoyed, he just wasn't very good.

So in February of his junior year in high school he tried out for the swimming team. From the beginning he was good, and his coach always believed he could be better, and kept showing him higher levels of achievement. In retrospect it would seem to Gaines that his rapid success was the result of "pure natural talent." By the end of his senior year in high school—only a year after he began swimming competitively—he was ranked ninth in the nation in the hundred free.

His parents never pushed him to excel in the sport, in part because they didn't know just how good he was. They had divorced a few years before; his mother had some idea of what a good time was in his events, his father had no idea, and Gaines preferred things that way.

In 1977, at the age of seventeen, he enrolled at Auburn University and began swimming for coach Richard Quick. Quick started him on weight training and "double workouts," training before school in the morning and again in the afternoon. During that first year at Auburn, he grew to be six-one, and weighed 160 pounds; by the middle of the summer he had become the premier sprint freestyler in America and placed second at the World Championships.

Over the next few years Gaines enjoyed an incredible collegiate swimming career, winning five NCAA titles and eleven National Championship titles. During those years he was excited about swimming. He enjoyed the press conferences, the attention, the excitement of setting world records; he liked the U.S. team trips, running down the hallways in hotels, having shaving cream fights, spending time with the other swimmers. He was naïve about his own success. It had happened so fast that he had no time to realize he was not the hunter anymore but the hunted, the favorite whom others would try to beat. While that naïveté lasted, swimming was a joy for him.

In 1980 he was favored to win a handful of gold medals in the Moscow Olympics, maybe five or even six with relays thrown in. That, he thought, would be the perfect cap for his short and glorious career. In 1977, as he entered Auburn, he had three goals: to win an NCAA title, to set a world record, and to win an Olympic gold medal. He had made two of those by 1980. But then there was the boycott.

The United States would send no team to the Moscow Olympics, in protest of the Soviet presence in Afghanistan.

Gaines wasn't the only one hurt. World record holders Tracy Caulkins, Steve Lundquist, and Bill Barrett, and American record holders Jeanne Childs, Sue Walsh, and Craig Beardsley, all at the peak of their careers, suddenly found their aspirations thwarted. That boycott had a profound effect on American swimming, reshaping the age distribution of stars in the sport and all but destroying the motivation of the top-rank athletes.

On Wednesday evening, January 4, 1984, two young men sat in plastic chairs at gate A 32 of the newly modernized Atlanta Hartsfield International Airport waiting for Delta Flight 321 to Austin, Texas. One of the men was Rowdy Gaines, coming from a family Christmas celebration in Winter Haven, Florida; the other was Tony Corbisiero from Queens, in New York City. Gaines was tall, thin, and loose-limbed, with blond hair; Corbisiero was short and stocky, with dark hair. The two sat and talked for an hour or so. Periodically, Gaines would stand up and walk over to the vending machine in the corridor and buy an ice cream sandwich, come back, and munch on it while they talked.

Both men were waiting for a plane to take them to another swim meet, with only six months to go until the Olympics. Things were different now than four years earlier. The Moscow boycott had made Gaines wary, hesitant to commit himself. At every meet he attended, the press people, attracted by Gaines' good looks, intelligence, maturity, and humor, kept asking him, *Will you be in Los Angeles?* He didn't really mind their asking all the time; that was their job, and he wasn't averse to getting some publicity, but he would dodge the questions: He wasn't sure, he'd have to see what happened. As he told it, he was having trouble supporting himself financially while trying to swim. U.S. Swimming gave him a grant of five hundred dollars a month, and he was living on that, mostly, doing maybe a few promotional things on the side; and although to some people (even friends) he denied actually having a press agent, he was certainly at least talking with sports promoters, and that was new and interesting. Swimming itself he now found less exciting. For one thing, he was as much as ten years older than other world-class swimmers. The horseplay in the hotels, the press conferences, the interviews didn't thrill him so much. There were other swimmers like him, older ones in their mid-twenties, Craig Beardsley, Jeanne Childs, Steve Lundquist, who, like Gaines, had kept swimming after college in hopes of finally going to the Olympic Games. There were havens for them, at the University of Florida and the University of Texas, where Gaines was now training with Richard Quick again, and with Eddie Reese.

Gaines' doubts seemed genuine. But in the water, in workouts, even with all his doubts (*I'm twenty-four years old. Why I am doing this every day?*), he pushed himself. Once in the water, he was fully committed.

Tony Corbisiero, his companion in the Atlanta airport waiting area, looked more like an undersized football player than a swimmer. He was outgoing, talkative, almost garrulous. Under Coach Ron Galuzzi of Columbia University, Corbisiero had become the first Ivy Leaguer in twenty years to win an NCAA swimming title. He was now training under Galuzzi's brother Lenny at Columbia, while Ron himself had moved to Ohio University. Corbisiero was psyched up for the international meet that he and Gaines were headed for. Corbisiero had even "tapered and shaved," dramatically reducing his work load in practice over the past few weeks ("tapering") so his body could recuperate its full energy, then shaving his arms, legs, chest, and back to provide a better "feel" for the water ("shaving"). These are standard rituals for serious swimmers, carried out perhaps three times a year, for the biggest meets. He had not done well at the summer Nationals, having placed in only the eight hundred, and now he felt that he had something to prove, to show people that they couldn't count him out. He was ready and confident. He had trained well that year.

In the spring of 1978, as an unknown freshman at Columbia, Corbisiero had placed fifth at NCAA's in the fifteen hundred. After the meet, Mark Schubert had written a letter to his coach, congratulating him on Corbisiero's success and suggesting that if Corbisiero would like to train long-course (in a fifty-meter pool) and with some outstanding competition, he might consider coming out to Mission Viejo for the summer season. Galuzzi showed the letter to Corbisiero, who was excited and flattered. So he packed up and went to California the first week of June 1978, boarded with a family in Mission Viejo, and started going to practices.

Corbisiero was at that time a top-rank distance swimmer whose specialty was swimming a mile at racing speed; he was faster at doing that than all but a handful of people in the world. He began his workouts at Mission, swimming in the Animal Lane. But he couldn't handle it. Physically, his body could not take the punishment of nine thousand meters in a practice, two practices a day, with no rest days. Within two weeks he had become completely exhausted by practices that were standard fare for the teenagers at Mission.

The first meet of the summer was the *Seventeen Magazine* Meet of Champions; Corbisiero was entered in the fifteen hundred. He didn't want to do it, he had no energy for doing it, but he dove in and swam anyway and did a terrible time, something over seventeen minutes. When he got out, one of the swimmers from the Mission team warned him to avoid Schubert, but Tony just went over to the warm-down pool to loosen up. He didn't feel good.

The next thing he knew, Schubert was at the edge of the pool, yelling at him to get out. Corbisiero climbed out. Then Schubert led him over in front of the stands, in front of the entire Mission team, in front of the hundreds of spectators in the stands, and there told him that he should never swim like that wearing a Mission Viejo suit, that he hadn't even tried. Corbisiero stood silent, on the verge of tears; no coach had ever yelled at him like this before. Schubert waved a sheet of paper with numbers written on it, pushed it into Corbisiero's hands, and told him to sit down on the deck and study the splits, the times he had done for each leg of the race. Corbisiero sat down right there where he was on the deck, and put his head down. Schubert turned and walked away. Corbisiero, shaken to his bones, stared at the sheet of paper.

It was a deliberate act on Schubert's part, not simply a fit of anger. Most kids would have bounced back, turning Schubert's anger in on their own performance, vowing never to give up like that again, and gaining in the process a fierce pride in being a Mission Viejo swimmer. But Corbisiero was not the average Mission Viejo swimmer. For one thing, he was older—he was already in college; and he was certainly not used to being treated this way by his coach, Ron Galuzzi. Too, Corbisiero had always been the star of his team, the biggest fish in the relatively small pond at Columbia. He came to Mission as a summer adventure; and he did not, it seemed to Schubert, make a total commitment to the program. Corbisiero was always—and perhaps it couldn't be helped—comparing Schubert with Galuzzi, Mission with Columbia, and concluding that this program didn't work for him, that his home coach didn't treat him this way. At least that was Schubert's analysis. Schubert felt afterward that he had simply made a mistake, but one that both he and Corbisiero would recognize and for which there were no hard feelings. The two, coach and swimmer, simply were not right for each other.

For the rest of the summer, Corbisiero feared that some little thing he might do would again set Schubert off into a rage. Corbisiero swam poorly that summer, and later he recalled hating every minute of it. After that weekend at the *Seventeen Magazine* Meet of Champions, he called home and talked with his parents. He cried as they talked, wondering aloud what he should do. His mother said, "Try a while longer, give it a chance," so he said, "Okay," and he stuck it out. The other swimmers helped him that summer. They told him not to mind what Schubert said, just to play the game: *Always be respectful, never question Mark in public. If you have a problem, talk with him about it in his office, but never challenge him in public.* In the office, one on one, Schubert seemed to listen and even to be reasonable, but in front of the team he was the absolute master.

For all his misery of that summer, Corbisiero still respected Schubert as a coach, respected his undeniable success in creating champions, such great swimmers as Marybeth Linzmeier and Tiffany Cohen and Brian Goodell and Jesse Vassallo. Corbisiero respected him for that, and sometimes even liked him a little, in a strange way. But he couldn't swim for him.

The next winter, Corbisiero went back to New York and trained with Galuzzi at Columbia again and did even better than the year before, placing second at NCAA's, which probably is the most competitive swim meet in the world. Again, Schubert called in the spring, despite the problems of the year before; and Corbisiero thought, *This year I can handle it, I know now what it is like, I can train in advance to prepare for the stress, now I can take it.* Again he went out to Mission, he boarded with a family there, and again, within weeks, he had broken down physically under the stress of nine thousand meters twice every day, the Animal Lane workouts. He tried taking one practice off each Wednesday morning, and Schubert let him this time; but then one day Schubert forgot the agreement, as Corbisiero remembers it, and yelled at him for not making that practice. Once Corbisiero missed a morning practice, just overslept. The phone rang, six o'clock in the morning it was; the owner of the house came in and said, *Tony, your best friend is on the phone.* Again he swam badly, again he was afraid, again he got yelled at. He went back to Galuzzi and the team at Columbia that winter and never returned to Mission Viejo.

In the summer of 1982, training in a little twenty-five-yard indoor pool with Galuzzi at Columbia, Tony Corbisiero went to the Nationals and broke the American record in the eight-hundred-meter freestyle.

As they sat in the airport, Gaines and Corbisiero flipped through a *Playboy,* and Gaines said that one of his little fantasies was someday to be the *Playboy* interviewee, and on the front cover would be the teaser, "Rowdy Gaines— Love, Sex, and Swimming," or something like that.

They boarded the plane to Austin at 5:45 P.M. Gaines sat in the front seat of the compartment, with his feet propped up on the partition separating coach from first class, his track shoes visible to passengers for a dozen rows back. The plane was delayed; then the stewardess came on the intercom and asked for volunteers to get off, since the flight was overbooked. Gaines' feet dropped, he spun around, and he looked back over the other passengers; several had decided to get off, and he joined them immediately. He was always up for something unusual, ready to step out of his usual schedule for a minor adventure. Besides, the free ticket that Delta offered him for his trouble would take him back to Florida in April for his sister's wedding. During the next few hours, while he waited for the next flight out, he talked football with ticket agents and janitors, made dollar bets with fellow passengers on the outcome of the AP football poll (Gaines loyally predicted that his alma mater, Auburn, would come out first; he lost the bets), and flirted with the young woman driving the golf cart that took him to the connecting flight gate. On the flight to Houston, he sat with a self-described "oilman" who swore like a sailor and promised Gaines some adventures with stewardesses at the hotel. Gaines politely declined. He could have worried that his late arrival into Austin might hurt his swimming, but he simply decided not to. That was typical. When he finally arrived, he was greeted by several coaches and friends who had come down to pick him up. He knew most of the top people in swimming, but major meets drew a crowd of others. Anytime he went to a meet—and this was to happen in Austin several times—a coach he didn't know would come up to him, a total stranger, and say, *Hey, Rowdy, how ya doing?* They would slap him on the back, shake his hand, and Gaines would genially play along, saying, *Hey, good to see ya,* even though he could not remember ever seeing this person before in his life. It was a little game that went with the territory, he knew, and it didn't really bother him much. For a world record holder, it was just part of the job.

Great accomplishments, we often assume, require heroic motivation: an intense desire to be the best, an inner strength beyond all measure, some special love of school, of family, of country. Some one of these must, we think, drive the superlative athlete.

Perhaps this comes from our own experiences in sport, where we discover now and then that great efforts are rewarded; one really can do much better than one had thought. So having had that experience—"I tried hard and did this well"—we seem to think that anyone who does so much better than we must have tried fantastically hard, or else have some magical "gift" or "talent." Movies and books encourage such views with tales of incredible comebacks and dramatic victories of the spirit; they try not so much for veracity as to be inspirational and perpetuate the sense of awe surrounding the great athlete.

This is an "heroic" conceit—a literary device, basically—and it actually does a terrible injustice to the athletes, for the heroic conceit mystifies excellence, removing it from the routines of daily life where it must, each day, be lived; it looks back over years and years of small events and tries to explain them in a quick phrase: "a career of excellence," "incredible dedication," "the will to win." So it fails, finally, to do justice to the drab routine of athletic training, and it presents dedication, too, as a gift—as something that one day you just "have" (like "talent"). In fact, world-class athletes get to the top level by making a thousand little decisions every morning and night. If you make the right choice on each of these—decide to get up and go to practice, decide to work hard today, decide to volunteer to do an extra event to help your team—then others will say you "have" dedication. But it is only the doing of those little things, all taken together, that makes that dedication. Great swimmers aren't made in the long run; they are made every day.

What *creates* champions is, first, the decision to stay in the sport and work hard. Perhaps nothing more heroic may be involved in this decision than habit ("I always go to practice in the morning"), boredom ("There's nothing else to do"), or commitments to friends ("Where were you yesterday?"). Swimmers like those from Mission Viejo are, in the sport, stars; they see their pictures in the hometown newspaper, they win varsity letters at school, they go on trips across the country and around the world. They get excused from school for a week at a time ("I'm going to Nationals"), and sometimes, if they win at a big meet like Nationals, they can stand up on a platform in front of three thousand cheering people and have photographers take their picture. Where else can a fourteen-year-old get that kind of attention?

CHAMPIONS

When Rowdy Gaines retired from swimming for a spring and summer, he found that there was no more excitement, no more glory; life was dull, and most of his friends were still going to workouts every day. So in a sense, excellence is built into the social world of top-rank swimming. Once you achieve that rank, that's where you find your friends, and as they get better, you have to keep up to stay in the group. As you find the rewards, you want to keep them. Even in this individual sport, the social ties are strong, created by the intensity of the daily workouts where five or six swimmers are packed together in a single lane. For years, Tiffany Cohen, Flo Barker, and Channon Hermstad have come to practice together; for years, Rowdy Gaines and Tony Corbisiero have been talking before meets. Some outsiders say that these athletes must have no friends, must be social outcasts. That misses the point completely. Their friends are what keep them in swimming.

Vidal Sassoon, Inc., the hairstyling people, had taken out a suite on the fourteenth floor of the Austin Hyatt Regency, the headquarters hotel for the U.S. Swimming International Meet. The Sassoon stylists—young women and men with New Wave haircuts, flashy makeup, and trendy clothes—had set up a combination styling boutique and TV lounge for sociable swimmers. Sassoon had recently come forward as a new national sponsor for U.S.S., and their people were here for the meet to do haircuts and makeovers (at no charge) for all U.S. National team members. Dara Torres was one of the first to get hers cut (she was always eager to try something new), and Mike O'Brien, whose hair was very short and neat already, had his cut again anyway. Every afternoon during the meet, after the preliminaries but before the evening finals, a crowd would gather up in the suite—Jeanne Childs, Kathy Treible, Torres, Mary Wayte—and hang around, watching the stylists at work, changing makeup, talking with whomever came through—parents, officials, or visitors. Grant Sainsbury, a friendly English photographer free-lancing for Sassoon, took pictures of some of the girls; some photos would later be run in *Seventeen Magazine* and *Gentlemen's Quarterly*. Sassoon wanted to advertise a new athletic haircut, the Aqua Cut, that together with waterproof makeup would ensure that "the swimmers were able to look good when competing."

The swimmers treated each other well; by and large, they *liked* each other. At the meet, and in the days before, when they were at the hotel, settling in and talking to the press, it resembled a high-school reunion. You can learn a lot about a group by finding what they consider bad manners. If you asked at the U.S.S. International meet what the swimmers and coaches considered bad manners, they had to think for a while; there seemed to be so little rudeness. "You don't see much," says Eddie Reese, the coach of the University of Texas team. But themes eventually emerge: It's bad manners to disrupt the warm-up by jumping in on people, or goofing around. It's rude to wave a fist in the air when you beat somebody; aggressive cheers are bad. In general, aggressiveness toward your opponents is real tacky, they say. Nobody here shaves their head, or throws a fit if they swim poorly. It's even bad manners to cry, with one exception: "Olympic Trials is an okay cry."

This is what is meant when we say that these swimmers are well mannered. But *why* is this so? Some athletes nowadays build a reputation for being impolite. Why, then, are these athletes so considerate of each other?

Swimmers work for five or more hours a day in close physical proximity to each other, in lanes where if one person gets out of line, the entire group is disrupted. Respect for others is necessary if any are to get their work done. It's a small world; they will be seeing their competitors over and over for years on end. Knowing that the relationships are long-term may encourage participants to be nice to each other.

Then, too there are very few spectators. The prestige one gains in swimming comes in the eyes of the other participants in swimming, athletes, and coaches. It is only with the addition of outside observers—at high-school and collegiate competitions, for instance—that the system of good manners begins to break down in sports. When hockey expanded into nonhockey towns and began playing for uninformed spectators, the game degenerated into brawls and violence. Swimming, being a nonspectator sport, has an inbred set of manners, played for the spectators who are there, one's competitors.

There are also no gains from verbal outbursts. In basketball, complaining against the referees can bring benefits, as the refs may become intimidated and then give more favorable calls. But in swimming, there is no such effect, because performance is unambiguous. No amount of either being nice or being nasty can change the time registered on a stopwatch. It is true that the officials are less likely to disqualify a major star, but even these situations are relatively rare.

The top-rank swimmers share the experiences and the challenges that come with speed in the water—of going to their first Junior Nationals, first Senior Nationals, first World Games, Olympic Trials, Olympics.

These common experiences transform the athletes into a cohesive group. On the team trips they get to know each other and become friends. So the good manners they display are not even that, not so well defined as "Good manners require that . . ." It's unconscious: This is just the way you act with friends and with professional colleagues. There's no book anywhere that tells swimmers how to behave at major meets. The courtesy shown within this top rank of club swimmers is the expression of the fact that they are a coherent group, not simply representatives of different teams, a group cut off from the rest of swimming and the rest of the world, with a shared past, similar abilities, and often a common dream.

Amid all the socializing at the Hyatt, one group of swimmers stood apart from the rest, and the Americans, especially the Mission Viejo distance freestyler Tiffany Cohen, who knew where the competition was, seemed always to be keeping an eye on them. They were the swimmers from the Deutsche Demokratische Republik, the D.D.R.— East Germany.

Few in number, tall in stature, distinctive in their sharp blue warm-up suits, the East Germans rarely spoke to swimmers from other nations and were rarely spoken to by those outside their group. They moved in small groups of two or three, usually accompanied by a coach or trainer. In contrast to the talkative, outgoing, laughing Japanese or the giggling young girls of West Germany, the East Germans were quiet, almost solemn in public. On the shuttle buses back and forth to the Texas Swimming Center, they sat in their own section of the bus, often one to a bench seat. They looked out the windows; and when they did talk with each other, it was quietly and always in German, never in English, which swimmers from other foreign nations would sometimes practice. Later in the evening at the Hyatt, they would stand in groups of four or five, wearing their blue warm-up suits, looking over the rail of the fourteenth floor of the Hyatt atrium, looking down at the people eating dinner in the restaurant on the ground floor, or maybe at the swimmers lining the rails on the floors below. The East Germans would point and talk among themselves but never with others; occasionally one or two of them, perhaps Ute Geweniger or Dirk Richter, would go down to the gift shop in the lobby and look through the postcards there. But they never wandered the streets of Austin and rarely traveled alone. They were intimidating by their very presence.

Their remarkably successful program is structured differently from that of American clubs. In the D.D.R., Olympic sports are run completely by the state. Sports clubs, officials, competitions—all are state-organized and state-sponsored. Participation is strongly encouraged and nearly universal. From a young age children are enrolled in the state-sponsored sports programs and participate in nationwide *Spartakiads*. In the early years of grade school, children with outstanding athletic potential are singled out; and once their parents have agreed, they join state-run sports academies to receive the finest available preparation for competition.

That preparation is highly technical and is based largely on the most developed sports medicine program in the world. Athletes are regularly monitored on their body composition, lactic acid tolerance, and oxygen-processing ability. Doctors are present at many workouts, and there is a very high coach/athlete ratio.

In the early years of their success, the East Germans were regularly accused in the American press of using anabolic steroids to build muscles and enhance performance. Over the years since, the view has emerged in U.S. Swimming that the "steroids" story is just an excuse for the weaker American performance and that in fact the East Germans' success is more likely due to the recruitment and development of all potential athletes and to highly individualized programs. Some knowledgeable Americans say that the East Germans do so well because for them, with a population of seventeen million, every athlete counts. When swimmer Peter Berndt, in 1985, became the first East German athlete to defect to the United States, one of his first complaints about American swimming programs would be the lack of individual attention. In the D.D.R., a coach would always stand near him with a stopwatch in hand during practices. By contrast, the American system often seems to be survival of the fittest, and Berndt found that he felt lost in a workout group of twenty or more. The close personal attention the East German athletes receive, as well as the substantial prestige and financial rewards, bring results: the finest Olympic-caliber athletes, per population, of any nation in the world. In the United States there is typically one Olympic gold medalist for every two million people in the country. In 1976, the last time there was a really competitive Olympics, East Germany claimed one gold medal for every 150,000 people.

The close supervision, of course, goes beyond the pool decks and sometimes appears restrictive. Once in a long while friendships will spring up between Americans and East Germans—at least among those who are of the top rank and so regularly see each other at meets. But letters are not exchanged, and the Americans are sometimes told by their counterparts not to bother writing. Still, some of the American swimmers like the East Germans, find them pleasant and even fun; but there is always the knowledge that no deep relationships can really develop.

Lawton Russell was able, in a way, to meet some East Germans. Russell, a genial, middle-aged employee of Transportation Enterprises, Inc., drove the shuttle bus to and from the pool and saw many of the athletes on those rides, although most of them hardly noticed him. Sometimes Russell, while stopped at a red light, would look at them in the rearview mirror. He thought, as he watched the West German teenagers, and the Americans, and the Japanese, that they aren't all that different, country to country. They may say this or that, in one language or another, but, as he sat and watched them, watched their eyes and their gestures, he could tell what each was like: Some were friendly, some were not; some told stories, and others just listened. When the East German girls in their blue warm-ups climbed onto the bus, they were usually stone silent. He wondered if maybe they were a little different from the rest, being from behind the Iron Curtain.

On Thursday morning, when he stopped at the Hyatt to pick them up, the East German girls were a few minutes late getting to the bus. When they finally came running out, they said something to him in words he couldn't understand, and gestured and smiled. Then one of them reached into the pocket of her warm-up jacket and took out a small gold lapel pin with the letters D.D.R. embossed on it. Russell later asked one of his American riders what the letters stood for, and he seemed all the more pleased when he learned. It was the sort of pin that athletes exchanged with one another as mementos of the meet, and she handed it to him with a smile and a few words in German. He thanked her; and throughout the day he would occasionally take it out of the pocket of his jacket and show it to any one of his passengers who had stopped and talked with him. He was proud of it. Later in the day he took the pin and, very carefully so as not to stick himself, put it on his shirt collar, and he wore it for the rest of the week.

For the American men, the East Germans as a team mattered little in Austin. For some reason—perhaps the Western world's less aggressive promotion of women in sports—the East Germans' advantage came largely through women's athletics; their men were more evenly matched by the rest of the world. Gaines, the American world record holder in the hundred free, came into the meet with something to prove—to show the world that his lackluster performance at the Pan Ams was just a slump. That summer was the first time in his life that he had failed to do any of his best times, and he wanted to do well at this meet. He did. In the hundred free, the event in which he held the world record, he led from the start (his usual pattern), and as the race went on, down and back the length of the fifty-meter pool, he pulled away, winning over Mike Heath of Florida with the comfortable time of 51.07 seconds. The race proved to Gaines (and, he hoped, to the press and his competitors) that he was back. Gaines had felt old the previous summer, the veteran of the team starting to slip, perhaps; but now he felt young again. In the locker room after the race, he overheard someone say that he, Rowdy Gaines, was tapered and shaved—that is, he had done special things to help his speed here, so his win wasn't that impressive. Rowdy thought, *Well, let them talk all they want; I know I'm doing well.* And though he didn't make the finals in the two-hundred free, swimming a little too slowly in the morning preliminaries, his time in the consolations was faster than that of the winner of the championship finals. In this meet he had swum the fastest two-hundred- and hundred-meter freestyles and the second-fastest fifty free. He was satisfied.

Tony Corbisiero, his companion from the airport, had also looked forward to the U.S.S. International. He had had a poor Nationals the previous summer and was an underdog here. Corbisiero was known as primarily a good short-course swimmer (better in the short twenty-five-yard pools used in college competition), so he, too, had something to prove. He did well at Austin, following his usual strategy of taking the race out fast. He took a first, a second, and a third and shared the high point trophy for the meet with Dirk Richter from the D.D.R.

For Mike O'Brien, the tall distance swimmer from Mission Viejo, the meet was wide open with the absence of the Russian world record holder in the distance events, Vladimir Salinokov, and of Jeff Kostoff, the dominant American distance swimmer. In the eight hundred on the opening day, O'Brien finished decently, with a respectable time in fourth place, behind the winner, Corbisiero, and two others. Then later, in the fifteen hundred, he used his formidable endurance to wear down the pack and win in

15:27, a good but not great time. O'Brien didn't have the need to win every race the way that some great swimmers do; he could look at a meet and think, "I'm in training now. What am I shooting for, really?" and point toward the big meets; he didn't get discouraged by doing less than brilliantly at minor meets.

Dara Torres did well, winning the fifty (as usual) and taking second in the hundred. She was even with East German Kristin Otto at the fifty, but Otto pulled away, eventually winning by a full second, a very clear victory in so short a race. Torres had maintained her speed better in the second half of the race than she had the year before—so, it seemed, the Mission Viejo program was giving her the endurance she needed.

In general the meet was presented by U.S.S. spokespeople and was seen by the press (and they were all there: reporters for *The New York Times*, *The Sporting News*, *USA Today*, *ESPN*, and the rest) as a victory for the American women. For the first time in years, they had competed with the East Germans on something like an equal footing, winning some events and at least challenging the East Germans in others. "America's Women Are Flying High Once More" announced *Sports Illustrated*, citing mainly the contributions of butterflyer Mary T. Meagher, who had been training for four months at Mission Viejo, and of Tracy Caulkins, the undisputed queen of American swimming. For weeks leading up to the meet, Caulkins had been plagued by a cyst under her left arm; with every stroke it rubbed and got sore. But now it had been drained and was healing, and she won both individual medley races against the D.D.R.'s Kathleen Nord, once by fifteen one-hundredths of a second and again by eighteen one-hundredths of a second. The times were not outstanding, and Nord was not really the best swimmer the Germans could have entered. But Caulkins was a deeply symbolic presence in American swimming, and when she won those races over an East

German in the presence of the noticeably partisan Texas crowd, she clearly staked her claim on the Phillips Performance Award given by the press for the outstanding race of the meet. *As Tracy Caulkins goes, so goes American women's swimming,* some people said, although realistically, Meagher's two-hundred butterfly swim probably was the better effort at the meet.

Caulkins was a kind of public property in swimming, winner of more national titles (forty-seven) than any other swimmer in history (including Johnny "Tarzan" Weismuller), and favored by the press for her intelligence and good looks. She was the only swimmer, male or female, ever to hold American records in all four strokes; she had been favored to win as many as four gold medals at the 1980 Olympics. Now, in 1984, at age twenty-one, she seemed past her physical peak, but she was still a factor in any race she entered, and was unchallenged in the United States in the medley events, which are comprised of all four competitive strokes.

But while the public could be convinced that American women were back, insiders knew better. Olympic Head Coach Don Gambril knew that Caulkins' victories were important but that her times weren't really that good; and he knew, too, that the East German women were heading into the Olympics with world record holders in three of the four strokes. Meagher, the butterflyer, was alone among the Americans in dominating her events. In the breaststroke, American women might be shut out of the finals completely, not even finishing in the top eight—a public-relations catastrophe. In addition, the D.D.R. kept producing great swimmers from out of the blue, turning over stars in rapid succession, so you never knew what they might come up with next. Their strategy of secrecy had some advantages that way. The Americans were in trouble, no question about it and Gambril told the press that, straight out.

But Gambril and the U.S. team would have some advantages, too. Foremost among these was that the Olympics would be held in Los Angeles, and there was always, even in swimming, a hometown advantage: the crowds cheering, and being accustomed to the food, the weather, the time schedule, and the pool. It had helped the Australian swimmers in 1956, and in 1968 Felipe Muñoz, in Mexico City, came from nowhere to become Mexico's first Olympic gold medalist, in the two-hundred-meter breaststroke. There would be strict drug testing, so *if* the East Germans or the Russians used steroids—and one Russian backstroker had been caught in a drug test at the 1978 World Championships—they would be disqualified by the officials.

The U.S. team had, in the past two years, changed from a men's team and a women's team into a combined squad, so that even in those meets where the women were losing badly, the men's victories could save face for the team. The *team* could claim some victories and so prop up the morale of the women swimmers. Those factors—drug testing, the home advantage, the combined teams—together with the prospect of some youngsters (for instance, Betsy Mitchell and Amy White in the backstroke events) coming up fast in the last six months before the Trials gave Gambril some hope that the American women might regain some of their badly tarnished prestige at the upcoming Olympics.

Off at the side of the University of Texas pool, standing and watching the U.S.S. International meet that January, was a smallish but muscular man, in his mid-thirties, perhaps, with light brown hair and a moustache. He seemed detached from what was going on, bemused almost. Every so often one of the swimmers would go up to him, get a friendly greeting, and stand chatting for five or ten minutes. They seemed to enjoy his company.

His name was Keith Bell. He was a former swimming coach and clincial psychologist, a Ph.D., who now spent his days writing books and pamphlets on sports psychology (*Championship Thinking, Winning Isn't Normal, Target on Gold*), and giving lectures and seminars on goal-setting and motivation. Bell himself is a marathon runner and a nationally ranked swimmer. He competed that year in the adult program of U.S. Swimming in the thirty-to-thirty-five age group; he would like someday to set a national record in the 1,650-yard freestyle, the longest racing distance. The fact that he trains and competes himself probably helped him to understand better what the athletes talking with him were feeling. All of them at the U.S.S. Nationals were tough, very tough, mentally, or they wouldn't have gotten to the meet in the first place. But they weren't perfect, and they wanted to be, so they came to Bell. Often, as he talked with swimmers, he would find that sometimes they would begin to imagine losing, what it might be like, what they would say to other people, and they brooded on it and imagined all of the details until, Bell realized, they might make it come true. He would try talking with some of the swimmers who thought about losing, would try in some little ways to distract them. Maybe he would tell a joke, or ask them about winning, would try to get them to think about doing well, to focus on that for a while.

The fear of losing, he found, was most prevalent in those who often had won in the past and who now feared letting down their coach, disappointing teammates, not living up to expectations. If they lost, the entire swimming world would see it. Sometimes, in giving talks to groups who really didn't understand the pressures of the sport, Bell would get up in front of the group and say, "I'll show you what swimmers go through," and there, on the platform, he'd strip down to a racing suit—1½ ounces of stretch nylon—and say, *Here I am, nearly naked, in public, in front of a huge crowd of people; I'm doing something that matters, and that (in swimming) will be evaluated to the hundredth of a second, and if I do poorly,* there's *absolutely no hiding or covering it up. Failure here is totally public. And if I say to myself, I won't try very hard, just in case I fail—then I haven't got a chance of succeeding.*

So Bell did what he could, standing on the deck of the Texas Swimming Center, to alleviate the pressure for the kids who would come over and talk with him before their races. They were scared, many of them, of what they were attempting and of the looming possibility of public failure. And this meet in Austin, Texas, was not the biggest meet of the year 1984, not at all.

7

Dress Rehearsal

ON TELEVISION, THE SPEED, THE GRACE, AND THE BEAUTY OF world-class competitive swimming goes flat and disappears. Telephoto lenses, collapsing vast distances into the shallow space of a television screen, collapse one's perception of speed as well. The grace, the ease with which a swimmer moves—slides—through the water is lost below the surface of the water, rendered invisible by the sun's reflection. Too often the beauty is lost as well because of the distance of the camera from the action; looking down from a height onto a field of eight competitors, one misses how one or two swimmers in particular seem to flow with an effortless power down the pool, moving many yards with each stroke. Their hands enter the water and begin to pull, and, in apparent defiance of the laws of physics, the hands seem to leave the water *ahead* of where they went in. The effect on a spectator can be startling, as is one's first exposure to a professional basketball game or world-class track meet: *My God, these people are huge, or they fly around the track.* At a swim meet they don't seem to be pulling or kicking, this isn't the "crawl" stroke—they flow and *slide* so smoothly and quickly it's uncanny, almost bizarre to watch. The television viewers get a hint, perhaps, of the speed of world-class swimmers only when the camera goes deck-level and moves along the side of the pool with the swimmers and see how the pavement on the edge of the screen seems to be moving very quickly. In a sprint, one would have to go at a slow run down the poolside to keep up.

But even if television could capture the realities of the swimming itself—the impressive length of an Olympic-size pool, the speed and beauty of the athletes in motion—viewers would still see only the surface of the race. Swimmers often complain that television coverage of the sport, when there is any, treats it like a horse race, with the focus on who's ahead and on how the stars are doing. They seem insulted by this. Somehow television suggests that the race itself is what counts, rather than it being a reflection, or a measure, of something else. The swimmers themselves find races, as such, boring. Swimmers at a big meet don't stand around watching the swimming. They talk with each other, warm up, get rubdowns, eat snacks, talk with coaches, and only sometimes watch the swim of a potential opponent or a friend.

Only when one knows the competitors, understands their styles, where they are in their careers and seasons, what they are trying to accomplish, does any of it make sense or hold interest. The inner drama of swimming meets emerges only when one moves among personalities and histories; television lacks the time for either; and so it inevitably distorts how we see each race and separates us from the people involved.

If each race has meaning only against a background, so, too, with each meet. Clearly the Olympic Games are a definitive meet; 1984 itself was called an "Olympic year," as if the aura of the week-long swimming competition in late July permeated the long months preceding it, giving that training period a purpose special beyond the training periods of other years. Throughout the Olympic year of 1984, coaches found their athletes more motivated, more willing to work hard in hopes of competing in Los Angeles. So in the spring of 1984, the National Championships were, as *Swimming World* subtitled its article covering them, "A Testing Ground" for Olympic prospects. Actually in an Olympic year, the Nationals had little importance in themselves: some great swimmers, in the middle of heavy training for Olympic Trials, would perform badly, and some new, unfamiliar people would win events. All that mattered was the preparation for the Olympic Trials (to make the team) and for the Games themselves.

So the 1984 Spring National Championship meet was designed, in all details, as a rehearsal for the Olympic Trials and the Games. The schedule of events matched that of the Olympics in time of day, order of events, and break time between preliminary heats and the finals. Following international rules, a gun would be used for the starting signal instead of the American-style electronic beeper. International rules require that a bell signal the last lap of the longer races, rather than the gunshot employed in American swimming, so a bell would be used. There would be a "ready room" where the eight finalists in each event would sit together for twenty minutes before the event began (a psychological horror that has unnerved many competitors); there would be urinalysis after the race to test for banned drugs; there would be only one antiturbulence lane line between lanes in the pool, instead of the usual luxury of two or three, because international rules would not accept world records set in pools with multiple lane lines. Finally, the meet would be held not in the traditional (for Americans) twenty-five-yard course but instead in the international standard fifty-meter pool at Indianapolis, where the Trials themselves would be held in June.

The length of the pool was crucial. The difference between racing in a short-course, or twenty-five-yard, pool and in a long-course, or fifty-meter, pool is something like the difference between playing a par-three pitch-and-putt golf course and playing the eighteen-hole championship course at Augusta, Georgia. The short-course pools feel faster, since one travels each lap so much more quickly. And they *are* faster, since one spends less time swimming through the water and more time pushing off the walls. Chance—the unpredictable vagaries of a start and a turn—counts for more. Different athletes excel in different-length pools.

The *long-course* races are, simply put, harder to swim than the *short-course* races. In any competition the serious swimmer will calculate his or her energy to run out, the body completely exhausted, at the exact moment of reaching the finish. A 50-meter pool, which is more than a dozen feet longer than fifty *yards*, thus destroys the swimmer's sense of pace of where he or she is. Even with the best goggles, vision is distorted underwater; you don't know when the end is coming. To a swimmer who has logged many thousands of hours in a short-course pool, the long-course pool feels like it will never end; the wall seems never to arrive. The delicate rhythm of twelve or fourteen strokes per lap, ingrained over hundreds of miles of training in a season, is suddenly broken, replaced only by the sensation of swimming in an endless lake. In the short sprints, breathing patterns must be changed: Whereas the great sprinters might normally take only one breath on the first lap (twenty-five yards) and two on the second (another twenty-five), now there is only a straight course (fifty yards plus), one lap with few visible indicators of where one is. Backstroke swimmers, looking for the pennants that hang over the ends of the pool five yards from the wall, find them moved back about a foot and a half, and the timing of the blind turns backstrokers must make while staring at the ceiling can be thrown off.

Finally, and perhaps most importantly, in a fifty-meter long-course pool there are fewer turns. The lazy swimmer loves the turns, a chance to stop pulling for a moment, to use the powerful leg extensor muscles, unused for most of the race, to push off against something solid. Turns provide a chance, in breaststroke and butterfly, to stop for an instant, take a full breath, and then go again. There are countless great short-course swimmers in America—great sprinters mainly, with fantastic turns—who never achieve distinction in long-course meets, and the big international meets are always held in long-course pools. People in the sport know the difference between a short-course swimmer and a long-course swimmer. At the Munich Olympics in 1972, a reporter asked Mark Spitz, then favored to win seven gold medals, if he was worried about the challenge from Dave Edgar, a very fast young freestyler from the University of Tennessee. Edgar at the time held the American record in the hundred-yard freestyle (*short course*), roughly equivalent to the Olympic hundred-meter free, and had been the dominant man during the indoor season. Spitz, with a background of years and years of long-course training in the fifty-meter pools of Santa Clara and Arden Hills near San Francisco, answered simply, "This is swimming, not turns."

The Olympics would be held in a long-course pool, so these Nationals would be held in one. The swimmers and coaches could then get some idea of how the course conversion would affect their performances. All that spring, swimmers and coaches had played with little hand-held slide-rule conversion charts, and looked at different time standards, and tried to guess what their times (in yards) would mean in meters; but the charts didn't work because of the turns, and besides, time standards hardly work at all because of the psychological impact of the longer pools. The swimmers came to Indianapolis in part to find out who would swim well and win over the long course.

The course conversion problem worried Don Gambril, the head coach for the Olympic team. As he watched the short-course college season, he saw that there were great swims from George DiCarlo and Jeff Kostoff in the distance freestyles. But how much did that mean? Tracy Caulkins certainly swam some great short-course times. But so what? The U.S.S. International Meet in the long-course pool at Austin had given some indications, but that was in midseason, and while some swimmers, like Tony Corbisiero and Rowdy Gaines, had tapered and shaved for that meet (and so were at a peak), many others had not reduced their work loads at all and so swam tired and slow: Who knew what they could really do? The mass of American swimming talent remained untested that year in long-course meets; and Coach Gambril, who felt responsible (and would be held publicly accountable) for the Americans' Olympic performances, was more than a little bit nervous.

Mark Schubert was not nervous. As always, he knew that by the time the meet started, the coach's job was largely over, and that he had dealt with the yards-to-meters problem. Hard training was the key to success; if the preparation was right, the performance would follow. His swimmers practiced gauging the pool length, sprinting out and hanging on, pacing the longer swims, racing an opponent, and finishing fast. He was well organized, and the strength of his program lay in the careful preparation for every possible contingency, both in and out of the water; as little as possible was left to chance.

The day before the swimmers left for the National Championships, yellow and blue Speedo team warm-up suits and caps and custom-designed Lycra racing suits with the words "Mission Viejo" woven right into the fabric were given out to the Nadadores. Speedo, the swimsuit company, a longtime sponsor of the Mission Viejo team, had donated all the equipment, and Schubert always reminded the swimmers to wear only Speedo gear—shirts, caps, even goggles—when at the meet.

The next morning at Orange County's John Wayne Airport, Assistant Coach Terry Stoddard handed out all the tickets, in alphabetical order, a few minutes before boarding. When the team arrived at the Indianapolis airport three hours later, vans and station wagons driven by coaches and chaperones were waiting to take the dozens of Mission Viejo swimmers to the Hyatt Hotel; at the Hyatt, keys to all the rooms (boys and girls on separate floors) were waiting. Every night the next day's schedule—wake-up swims at six-fifteen, breakfast at seven-thirty, the van to the pool for prelim heats at nine—was posted on all the staff members' doors; at team meetings every afternoon times were announced, performances noted, arrangements made. All day long, cars and vans, leaving their stops punctually every fifteen minutes, shuttled the swimmers from the Hyatt to the pool and back again, going over for prelims and finals, and then back to the hotel for rest and meals.

For all meals, the swimmers checked in at one of the hotel's banquet rooms (as noted on the schedules), signed the list kept by one of the staff, and dined at a buffet specially prepared for the team. The menus were carefully planned—low in fat, high in carbohydrates, with lots of vegetables. In one team meeting Schubert remarked on the excess of butter on the carrots and made a note to speak with the food manager. At dinner one night Mike O'Brien pointed out to the younger, perhaps less conscientious swimmers at his table that milk, having a high fat content, "is a condiment," to be used sparingly, and only skim milk at that. Diane Johnson, one of the older and wiser swimmers, would refuse sugary granola bars for snacks and eat rice cakes (low in fat, high in carbohydrates) instead; and if Dara Torres ate ice cream on the sly, that was typical only of Dara Torres, not of the team in general.

Their appetites were considerable. One night at the Nationals, the Hyatt waiters had to bring out tray after tray of lasagna; the first one was gone in less than a minute, and the waiter had to explain to an incredulous food manager, "We didn't think they'd eat this much." Butterflyer Mary T. Meagher—to mention but one example on the team—downed several salads, a mug of her favorite brand of instant-mix hot chocolate (which she brought to every meal), and three full plates of lasagna. At the time this was happening, across the atrium at The Porch restaurant, U.S.S. Technical Director Selden Fritschner was just sitting down to dinner with a friend. He ordered lasagna and was told that there was none left; the Mission Viejo team had eaten it all.

Even with some sixty swimmers at the meet—easily the largest roster of any single club—the Mission Viejo organization ran with surprising efficiency. There were a half dozen or so of the staff people giving rubdowns at the pool (on massage tables behind the diving boards) or at the hotel. The Mission staff people were all easily recognized at the meet, wearing the same color shirts with "Mission Viejo" on the breast. The shirt colors changed daily: blue on Monday, white on Tuesday, yellow on Wednesday, and so on. They knew, too, that should any of the coaches or staff go out to a bar in the evening, they would wear their own shirt, not a Mission Viejo shirt. At night there was a room check and then, half an hour later, a bed check to make sure that everyone on the team was in bed, lights out, early enough for a good night's sleep. Older swimmers, those of college age, found such rules to be a humiliation. But "the best way I know to get sick," Schubert said to the team at the end of the meet, "is to stay up late the last night after the meet, then get up at five-thirty in the morning to catch a plane back to Orange County." Even then he was preparing for the Olympic Trials two months later.

Other teams were different. Other swimmers made their own travel plans, checked into their motels alone or in small groups, ate their meals at McDonald's or in the hotel restaurant or even in their rooms, using hot plates and eating (literally) Campbell's soup and crackers. Those too old—too proud, perhaps—to be supported by their parents, especially victims of the 1980 boycott, were amateurs still, with only (and this if they were lucky) a five-hundred-dollar monthly grant from U.S. Swimming, or an Olympic Jobs Program position with Anheuser-Busch. At meets they argued over whether to walk to the pool or rent a car; taxis might in the long run be more expensive than renting; some managed, occasionally, to hitch rides with the larger teams that had cars.

Some of those other teams resented the Mission team's organization and financing—always staying in the Hyatt, in rooms rated at ninety-five dollars a night; eating all specially prepared meals, in a team dining room; the shuttle vans, the rubdown staff, sometimes a professional trainer. Mission always got all the perks. On the plane from Orange County—the plane was filled with swimmers from many teams, not just Mission—the stewardess came on the public-address system and welcomed all the Mission Viejo Nadadores and wished them luck at the Nationals. Other teams resented the money and the attention; yet many said, too, that they could never swim on a team or under a coach who controlled so much.

"Some people don't approve of Mark's methods," said one of the parents who went to Nationals as a chaperone, "but I'll say one thing: He really does take care of these kids . . . getting them fed, housed, transported to the pool." His kids dove into the water knowing they had nothing to think about save swimming. Everything else was provided.

Dress Rehearsal

*   *   *

The Mission Viejo team boasted one impressive new member at this meet. For five years, Mary T. Meagher (the name is pronounced with a silent g, as "Mah-her") had been the dominant woman butterfly swimmer in the world, the uncontested "best ever" in the most grueling stroke in swimming. Even in international meets, she often finished the two-hundred-meter race more than five seconds ahead of the second-place finisher.

She had spent most of her life in competitive swimming. She began at five years old, swimming on a country club team in a summer league in her hometown of Louisville, Kentucky, where she grew up as the tenth of eleven children. Her father owned a hardware store; her mother (whose maiden name, Terstegge, provided the "T" in "Mary T.") raised the kids. Mary swam on the summer team until she was nine, when she began practicing—more seriously, now—with the Plantation Country Club team, which competed year-round in AAU meets against other teams in the Southeast. In those years (the mid-seventies) the region was becoming a national swimming hotbed, with the Nashville appearance of the young Tracy Caulkins and Joan Pennington. From the beginning, Meagher was very competitive, and after moving to the Plantation team she improved quickly. By her thirteenth birthday she was good enough to swim at the National Championships in the butterfly events. Looking for new challenges, she changed teams again (this would be her habit, always looking for the right coach for each stage of her career) and went across town to the Lakeside Aquatics team, coached by an ambitious young man named Denny Pursley.

Pursley quickly saw Meagher's talent for swimming the butterfly very smoothly, with her hips—and this is a sign that coaches look for, a very unusual sign—always staying near the top of the water, so that she was lying prone on her stomach, nearly flat, not bouncing up and down the way most swimmers do. In the butterfly, both arms sweep forward across the water simultaneously; then the pull is made; and the arms are again lifted out of the water at the same time, and they sweep forward again. For the novice, the stroke is terribly exhausting; with every stroke, the body sinks lower and lower in the water, until the swimmer is left struggling just to get up and get a breath. It seems, on first effort, a grossly unnatural way to travel down a pool. But for Meagher the stroke was natural: Her arms flowed forward, they pulled back underneath her, and they swept forward again. Her body never sank; her hips were always near the top of the water. This feature of her stroke remained a hallmark for the rest of her career, a sign that separated her from others in the races she swam, even against the best competition in the world: Her hips never sink.

Pursley saw this, and saw, too, that Meagher could swim the butterfly for hours without her technique deteriorating, and he thought that she could place much higher than thirteenth at Nationals, her best finish that year. So he took her aside and told her that if she wanted to swim for him, she had to make a total commitment: She would stop playing softball, stop cheerleading, stop basketball; she would give up all other sports, and she would build her life around swimming—not only in the pool, not just during practice, but all the time. She would be so tired, even on weekends, that she wouldn't want to do anything but rest up for the next workout. Meagher, thirteen years old, talked it over with her parents, who barely understood how good their child was at this sport, and they all agreed that if her coach thought she could do that well, she should try it. So she did.

Pursley told her, first, that she must never be late to practice. Every day after school, Mrs. Meagher would pick up Mary T. (her family and friends just call her "T.") at school and they would rush through the streets of

Louisville, hoping to hit all of the lights so she would make it to practice on time. Pursley accepted no excuses, however legitimate, and late arrivals had to stay fifteen minutes after the workout. Sometimes, when there were too many red lights, when Mrs. Meagher couldn't drive fast enough to make up the time, Mary T. would sit in the car quietly crying to herself, knowing they wouldn't make it. Pursley also began making her swim continuous butterfly sets, with no freestyle thrown in to make the workout a bit easier, nothing but butterfly; and she swam with a rubber tube around her ankles to make it more difficult, and with large plastic paddles on her hands, to build her muscles still more; and she began lifting weights to fill out her still-skinny arms. He told her, *You can't just train hard; everybody trains hard: Look around, see how the others train, and train harder than they do.* For the last half hour of the practice, Pursley kept only the butterflyers—the "flyers," swimmers say—so there was plenty of space for the wide arm strokes over the water, and he made them swim another half hour of butterfly. Mary T. Meagher led them all.

It seemed to Pursley, when some years later he looked back on that time, that Meagher's great advantage as a competitor was that her family, her religious beliefs (she was an active, practicing Catholic), and her life were all more important to her than swimming. So a disappointing performance was always only a poor swim and no more, not a reflection on her worth as a human being. She could go all out without fearing the possibility of a loss.

At the end of that year of commitment, in the summer of 1979, Mary T. Meagher, braces on teeth and stuffed frog "Bubbles" in arms, stood on the victory platform and waved to the crowd at the Pan American Games in San Juan, Puerto Rico, as the announcer told them that she had broken the world record in the two-hundred-meter butterfly.

Meagher and her parents were remarkably naïve about her success, failing to see the forest for the trees. They

Mark Schubert after the 1976 Montreal Olympics, with his swimmers Brian Good-ell (two gold medals) and Shirley Babashoff (four silver medals and one gold). Only twenty-six years old, Schubert was a bit unsure of himself, concerned with maintaining authority over his athletes.

Some of the Mission Viejo girls in an afternoon training session in the Marguerite pool. Far from being a truly individual sport, competitive swimming is an emotionally intense experience shared with friends, and the social sacrifices of training are usually overstated. **Daniel F. Chambliss**

Ambrose "Rowdy" Gaines IV during a warmup at the University of Texas pool, January 1983. At twenty-four, he often thought of retiring from the sport, wondering if perhaps he wasn't too old for swimming. **Daniel F. Chambliss**

In 1979, Mary T. Meagher, only fourteen years old, swam the two-hundred-meter butterfly event at the Pan American Games in San Juan, Puerto Rico, and broke the world record. To her family and close friends she was "T"; to coaches and other swimmers she was "Mary T." The press called her "Madame Butterfly." **Tony Duffy/AllSport**

Dara Torres practicing her freestyle, 1984. **Daniel F. Chambliss**

Mike O'Brien dries off after a swim at the Olympic trials in Indianapolis, 1984. By Saturday, the final day of the meet, he would have only one chance remaining to make the U.S. team. **Daniel F. Chambliss**

Dara Torres, arguably the best pure sprinter in the world. She wears a custom-knitted "Mission Viejo" racing suit. **Tony Duffy/AllSport**

Rowdy Gaines, Olympic gold medalist in the one-hundred-meter freestyle. **Tony Duffy/AllSport**

The American women lead the field in the four-hundred-meter freestyle relay at the 1984 Olympic games. **Gary Morris**

Channon Hermstad—"Hermie," to her friends—a core member of the Mission Viejo team. She is wearing a Ricardo Prado T-shirt from a clinic "Reeky" ran in his home country of Brazil. Behind her the team stretches out before a workout. **Daniel F. Chambliss**

Mike O'Brien in one of many close
races. **Mike Powell/AllSport**

Dara Torres and friend Kim Brown at the Nationals, 1986. Torres had always loved the
photographers, and they loved her. **Tony
Duffy/AllSport**

By 1987, Meagher was a senior at the University of California at Berkeley, a seventeen-year veteran of competitive swimming, a grown woman, and still holder of both world records in the butterfly. She would be favored to win two gold medals at the 1988 Olympics in Seoul, South Korea. **University of California Sports Information**

Mike O'Brien, only eighteen years old, on the victory stand. *Swimming World* called him "Mr. Clean." **Tony Duffy/All-Sport**

Mark Schubert at Mission Viejo in 1985. He was older now, and more confident. By 1986, his team had won forty-four national team championships, more than any other team in swimming history. He was at the pinnacle of his profession, a coach of champions. **Tony Duffy/AllSport**

knew that she had to be on time for practice and that she had to swim the strokes legally throughout the workouts; they knew she stayed for the extra thirty minutes every day to swim 'fly; and they knew she was getting faster. But Mary T. herself had really never thought about the Olympic Games, or winning a gold medal, or even breaking the world record as specific goals. In fact, at San Juan, when she did break the record, she wasn't even aware of it until five minutes afterward, when someone came over and congratulated her. She had just listened to the coach, all throughout her career. The coach would say, *There's this meet called Regionals, you should swim in it*, and she would; or *There's this meet called National Junior Olympics, you should swim there*, and she would, thinking how much fun it was to be this little squirt who'd swim against big kids and beat them. She didn't think about making Junior Olympics, or making Nationals as a goal in itself. The world record, from her point of view, just followed naturally.

Her parents were less aware than Mary T. of what was happening. They were involved with all of their children (eleven of them, remember), with Girl Scouts and car pools and more; when Mary T. broke the world record, she was the center of attention for a week, perhaps, but then an older sister would have a baby, another sister would graduate from law school, and the family would turn their attention away. Occasionally Mrs. Meagher would come to a swimming meet and watch, sitting with her hands folded in her lap, her legs crossed, happy for her child, but bored nonetheless by the endless events of a swimming meet. If Mary T. would tell her a time she'd just swum, Mrs. Meagher would say something like, "That's nice, dear," but if the times weren't so good, she just didn't know it. Mr. and Mrs. Meagher were surprised when Mary T. had her expenses paid on a trip to California, when she was first becoming good enough to qualify for the athlete support program of U.S.S.; and they didn't know the names of any other big swimmers, although after the first world record they did start a subscription to *Swimming World* magazine.

It was a blessing, Meagher would realize later, that her parents were so naïve. She never felt any pressure from home to swim or break records; once she had decided to join the team for a season, they would make her stick with it, and not give up when the workouts became demanding, but they didn't make her swim. Years later, when she was an authentic star in the sport—a celebrity, really—she would be saddened when parents came to her and asked, *Where should my child go to train? Should my child stop playing field hockey? Here are my child's times. Is she ahead of where you were?* She resolved that when she married and had children of her own she would never do that, she would never force the sport on them, or try to manage her children's lives. She hoped to be as good a parent as her parents had been.

After breaking a string of world records in the years 1979–81, and after the frustration of the 1980 Olympic boycott (although it seemed to hurt her less than it did some of the others) she was ready for a break from swimming. Once before, just after the 1979 records, she had thought about quitting the sport, she was tired of all the workouts; but now she did it. She started playing field hockey again at school and began looking at colleges. Swimming would not be the prime consideration; there were academic factors, and social ones as well. She finally settled on the University of California at Berkeley, in part because it is a top-rank academic institution, in part because there was a good women's swimming program, in part for the social scene. For her entire life Meagher had attended Catholic schools, most recently having graduated from Sacred Heart Academy in Louisville. True, she had never been interested in drinking, drugs, smoking, and wild parties, and she didn't plan on going to Cal to break loose; but it is a huge university, and people there don't care what you wear to class, and they don't know you unless you want them to (even if you are a world record holder), and Mary T. Meagher liked that, the anonymity she might find. At Cal, she discovered, her athletic accomplishments didn't mean that much; all that people seemed to care about was whether you were a Democrat or a Republican. She liked it. She joined the Order of the Golden Bear, a kind of booster club, and they discussed the university's public image, and the divestment movement, and the role of sports in the university, and she went to parties and took a major in child development. Her athletic training naturally fell off a bit, she gained some weight, she worked out much less often. She still swam on the college team and did very well, winning a number of NCAA championship titles; and that was fine with her, for the time being.

In the fall of 1983, though, she saw another Olympic Games coming up, this time in Los Angeles, and she decided to commit herself fully once again to swimming. She left Berkeley for a year and headed for Orange County, California, to join the team and the coach that would most likely give her the training, the discipline, and the competition in workouts she needed to win in the Olympic Games—the Mission Viejo Nadadores. She was by then eighteen years old, an attractive young woman with dark brown hair cut short, and an open, pleasant face; she was intelligent and articulate, mature beyond her years. In the early years she had been the kid who came out of Louisville to beat the world; now she was the veteran, the clear favorite in the butterfly events, American's only "sure" gold medalist for Los Angeles. She now had more to lose, since now the expectations were so high, but she still gave the impression that swimming, while important, was not the only thing in her life.

From the first few days in the fall of 1983, she was a

leader on the Mission team. Soon, even before she was eligible under U.S.S. rules to represent Mission Viejo officially in competitions, her teammates elected her captain of the team. The honor came in part because she was a great athlete, but there were other reasons. Her teammates respected Meagher for being a star who worked hard— even though she could have loafed through practices and still won—a woman who challenged herself and supported her teammates. When in March 1984 the team attended the Spring Nationals, Mark Schubert asked her to take charge of organizing the team's meal service at the Hyatt. She took the job seriously. She and Mike O'Brien, the tall distance freestyle swimmer, designed menus for the week, negotiated the entire package with the food service manager of the Hyatt, and worked out the times and the prices and the service details. When there were little snags or minor complaints, Meagher would speak to the manager and solve the problem.

Then every night, after the team had eaten dinner in the mezzanine overlooking the atrium of the Indianapolis Hyatt, while a small swing band played dance music in the lobby down below, Meagher would sit for an hour or two at the table, as waiters cleared away the dishes, and talk with different people on the team, swimmers from around the world. She talked for hours with one, Andy Astbury, a British fellow who had come to the United States to swim at Arizona State University. Meagher liked him because they were, these two swimmers, so alike yet so different. They talked about their countries and their schools, and they laughed about differences between ASU, where fraternities ruled and the dorms were single-sex, and Cal, where the political debates were vigorous and the dorms were coed. She loved talking with people, and they loved talking with her.

At Indianapolis it seemed that what made this huge group of swimmers a team was the organization of meals, rooms, trips, and transportation to the pool. Many had only recently joined the team, and a fair number flew to Indianapolis from such colleges as Arkansas or Harvard to score points for the Mission team. This was no team in the traditional sense of a stable group with a long shared history of goals, victories, and defeats. Except for a core of veterans—Mike O'Brien, Tiffany Cohen, Florence Barker, Channon Hermstad, and a few others—Mission was a collection of college students coming back to help out, and small-team stars who wanted to see if they could make it in the big time, which for most swimmers out in the provinces meant: Going to Mission Viejo.

Each night at dinner a main item of conversation was who the new people were. "What's the name of that guy who does IM [individual medley]?" "Where are you from?" "Iowa," came one answer. Or "Auburn"—like Mike Bream in the sprint freestyles; or "Israel"—like Hadar Rubenstein in the butterfly; or "New Zealand"—like Paul Kingsman in the backstroke. When Kingsman, who would stay with the Nadadores through the Olympics, made the finals in the two-hundred backstroke, Mark Schubert read his name at the team meeting—the finals sheet read "Kingman," without the "s," and Schubert read it and thought a minute and then said, "They spelled your name wrong." But even Schubert had to think about it first, to be sure what the name was.

They weren't recruited. Recruiting was hardly necessary, given the team's visibility. Every year hundreds of letters came into Martha Lee Pyykko's office at the Marguerite pool asking about the program, about how to join, whether they could come visit, how to get to swim at Mission. Now, in the Olympic year, there was a last-minute scramble, especially by distance swimmers, to get on the Mission team, to get that serious all-out training that might give one the edge to make the Olympic team. Going to Mission was a statement that one really wanted to be the best, was willing to make a total commitment—to put up with the aggravation, the stress, the competition at practice, and to put up with Schubert's domination of one's life.

In the early days, Schubert would accept anyone willing to do the work he demanded, good swimmer or not. Gradually, as the team improved, his standards rose. At first he had accepted only Senior Nationals qualifiers; later you had to have a shot at scoring. Now he tended, especially in the summertime, to take only people who were sure to score and even likely to win at Nationals. Some of the college swimmers at the spring Nationals in Indy said they were drawn by the belief that the company would pay expenses for any swimmer who came and swam for Mission in the Nationals, but all had either been Nadadores in high school or had committed themselves to training with Schubert during the coming summer.

As the meet went on, day by day, fewer swimmers came to the team meals in the Hyatt meeting rooms, joking they might not place and would have to pay for all the meals, which were expensive; comments circulated about living on yogurt and crackers the last few days, or just going down to McDonald's. Only the best swimmers had everything taken care of, so it paid to be fast.

So if there was a *team* here, it consisted of swimmers who came to the Nationals for a variety of reasons and wore the Mission Viejo suit, rather than a group that had spent years training together. But it worked, since swimming is essentially a sport of individuals swimming their own races, with little real need to work closely with others. Individuals set records, and individuals win medals, and great individual swimmers do, occasionally, come from average teams. (This was the case with Steve Lundquist, a great swimmer who swam with only moderately good teams.)

Some swimmers at Mission were, of course, more a part of the team than were others. When Channon Hermstad stepped up onto the starting blocks for the four-hundred individual medley final, the others in the core group would chant and yell and cheer "Go, Hermie!"; when Amy White swam the hundred-meter backstroke, a group stood at the end of the pool waving their team towels and yelling; when Mary T. Meagher—the team captain—won the two-hundred-meter freestyle, the entire Mission team erupted into enthusiastic cheering. These girls, along with Florence Barker and a few of the boys, like Dave Louden and Frank Iacano and Mike O'Brien, formed the center of the team; around them clustered the college swimmers and the neophytes from the YMCA teams. They were the real Mission Viejo Nadadores.

For this core group, the high point at Spring Nationals may well have been when Channon Hermstad swam that four-hundred IM final. One day before, Hermstad had lost a close two-hundred breaststroke race to Jeanne Childs, to the sorrow of those who had seen her struggle, just short of stardom, for years. During that race, Mission Assistant Coach Walt Schlueter, a man well into his seventies, stood on the deck waving his arms and shouting, "Go, baby, go!" Mark Schubert bellowed "Go, Hermie!" time and again. They wanted so badly for her to win. But Childs had the stronger kick and won by a touch, leaving Hermstad, for the time being, only the second-best breaststroker in America. Now, one night later, heavy favorite Tracy Caulkins, discouraged by a mediocre preliminary time, had removed herself from the final. Pulling ahead of the field in the third quarter of the race—the breaststroke leg—Hermstad won the four-hundred-meter individual medley, taking her first National title. It seemed then that she might be able to take second to Caulkins at Trials and make the U.S. Olympic team. That prospect excited other swimmers on the Mission team. Hermstad was a regular, a hard-working swimmer who perhaps lacked the raw talent of the stars, and they began to think if Channon Hermstad had a shot at the Olympic team, perhaps they did as well. Her performance was a good omen.

Mary T. Meagher, as expected, won both the butterfly events, leaving the field well behind, and then surprised everyone by coming from behind and taking the two-hundred free. The harder training at Mission had paid off.

Dara Torres, suffering for several weeks from a sinus infection, won the fifty free; but in the preliminaries of the hundred she missed her turn and faded badly, finishing seventeenth—one place out of the consolation finals. For several hours officials disputed whether Tammy Thomas, who qualified a few places ahead of Torres, might fail to verify her meet entry time and thus be disqualified, but in the end her time was approved. So Torres had failed to qualify even for the consolation final in her only potential Olympic event.

Mike O'Brien had not shaved for the meet, since he was looking ahead to the Olympic Trials. He struggled to eighth place in the eight-hundred free and fifteenth in the four-hundred free. In the fifteen hundred—the metric mile, which he considered his best event—he finished in ninth place. In the four-hundred individual medley he placed an abysmal twenty-second. It was a fitting performance in a mostly mediocre meet.

As everyone expected, Mission Viejo won the combined (men's and women's) National team title, the fifteenth time that had happened (there are two Nationals a year, an indoor and an outdoor). With sixty-one swimmers at the meet, they scored 1,242½ points, nearly twice as many as runner-up Florida Aquatics. They piled up relay points, entering as many as four teams (and sometimes scoring with all four) in an event. The women won ten of seventeen events, and with leaders like Tiffany Cohen (who won two events) and Mary T. Meagher (who won three), they swept away the competition. Perhaps more impressive was the fact that the Mission Viejo men, despite having no one finish among the top six individual scorers for the meet, and despite neither winning nor taking second in a single individual event, nevertheless won the team title. Like the women, they piled up relay points and qualified four and five swimmers in the finals of the distance freestyles and medleys. Schubert's consistent strategy of getting the most people in the water, with the best distance training behind them, continued to get predictable results.

In the two-hundred-meter freestyle, Rowdy Gaines of Longhorn Aquatics took third behind Mike Heath and Bruce Hayes. It was Heath's first National title. A mainstay of the University of Florida team during the winter, Heath seemed to Gaines to be a fast-rising star and certainly a powerful threat in the two hundred. Afterward, Gaines said, "If I sit here and think about that race, I'll quit. . . . I still feel like I can win this event in the Olympics. Mentally, I was up; but physically, it wasn't there. I couldn't get home. I may skip the fifty and go home after this." But he didn't.

Later in the meet, Gaines won the hundred-meter freestyle, swimming his fastest time since he had broken the world record three years before.

PART III

8

Altered Images

DURING NATIONALS THEY WERE EVERYWHERE; COLORFULLY dressed swimmers filled every corner of the IUPUI (Indiana University/Purdue University at Indianapolis) Natatorium. Some were on the pool deck, some in the showers, some in the locker rooms, some outside in the hallways looking around, some talking together or joking or lying down in the stands, resting for an event. Others were swimming in the competition pool, loosening up in the diving well, or practicing turns in the fifty-meter warm-up pool off the far end of the competition course.

There were dozens of coaches, too, many of whom had only one or two swimmers at the meet. Trying to look busy, they checked stopwatches, skimmed heat sheets, collared one of the "name" coaches like Mark Schubert or Don Gambril or Randy Reese, asking for pointers or making small talk. There were swimsuit salespeople making their pitch, reporters wandering about, and photographers setting up by the end of the pool, looking for that one great shot. Visually, major swim meets approach a quiet kind of chaos. Only the officials, dressed in white and moving almost in unison, and the races themselves—eight swimmers in a line, going down the pool and back, almost together— seemed neat and clean.

That image soon would change. For most of each four-year Olympic cycle, only insiders care about this sport. Meets are covered by only a few sports magazines, only two or three events from Nationals are shown on TV, only a few hundred people are present in the stands, and only *Swimming World* prints the full meet results. Before the disruption of the Olympic summer the sport is run by insiders: a few longtime officials; a handful of coaches; a smattering of respected, older athletes; and that most venerable insider of all, tradition. They determine the meet format. They decide the scheduling of events and the rules that apply, the type of coverage given, and even, somehow, the reputations that emerge from the welter of final results. So the participants are pretty much allowed to do as they please, go where they like during the meets, and generally wander around and socialize. In this amateur sport, where athletes and officials are volunteers and most coaches are only meagerly paid, power is relatively diffuse; there is no clear focus of authority or action. Among those insiders, the people who had been involved with swimming for years, there are certainly arguments, divergent interests, but those interests never conflict too violently. In this small community, where most of the people call each other by first names, problems often are settled informally.

But for the next few months, swimming would be dominated not by the insiders of the sport but by outsiders, specifically by the organizers of the Los Angeles Olympic Games, and more generally by the millions of people who would watch the Games on television and whose taste in sports would shape what ABC showed them. The sport's image would be created by the cameramen, the commentators, the directors in television, and by newspaper reporters and writers for such magazines as *Sports Illustrated*. This was new in swimming. In professional football (for example) and basketball, schedules were changed, games postponed, time-outs taken all for the benefit of the networks and their advertisers; entire seasons were designed with fans in mind. Since swimming had been mostly a minor sport, the swimming community was used to running things in its own way.

But lately, in an effort to appeal to the journalists and the public they would speak to, U.S. Swimming officials tried to jazz up the show a little, to make swim meets— sometimes boring even to their participants—lively public spectacles. At the Nationals during the warm-up sessions before finals, a swing band would play the theme from *Rocky* or *Chariots of Fire*. There was the parade of the officials, marching out dressed in white. There were runners—teenage girls in khaki pants and red shirts who ran errands for the officials and were just generally around, ready to help, out on the pool deck—and a synchronized swimming group that pulled a huge flag across the pool while the swing band played "The Star-Spangled Banner." An announcer welcomed everyone and introduced all the finalists, who would stand on the blocks and wave to the crowd before their events. There were a few *U!S!A!, U!S!A!* chants that never really got off the ground, and awards ceremonies with a huge platform for the winners, and flowers and certificates and more waves to the crowd, all performed for the two hundred or so people scattered throughout the huge grandstands. In fact, there were far fewer people in the stands than actually competing in the meet or working on the deck. To an even mildly cynical observer the elaborate staging and big production numbers looked a little bit silly.

To add to the problems, most sportswriters who covered swimming were in the profession because they enjoyed football or basketball, not because they got excited watching five-day swim meets. On any day at Nationals, many of the reporters could be found in the press room watching NCAA basketball on television. There were only a few exceptions. John Weyler of the *Los Angeles Times* understood swimming and cared about it, saw that it differed from football or basketball in, for example, the physically demanding, year-round work required, or in the way most swimmers actually enjoyed the long hours of training. Craig Neff of *Sports Illustrated* knew something about swimming. With a longer lead time than the newspaper writers and a more sophisticated audience than the television reporters, Neff often sat for hours at a time talking with a swimmer or coach, really listening to what they had to tell him; his articles reflected that he was among the better swimming writers, and with a platform like *Sports Illustrated* he was perhaps the most widely read in America. This is not to say that he knew the most—that might be Bill Bell, who worked for *Swimming World*, or Weyler, whose daily couldn't devote that much space to swimming—but he was very good.

The swimmers appreciated Neff's articles, but even he made mistakes. Rick Carey, then the world record holder in the backstroke, read an article about himself in *Sports Illustrated* and said, "It's a really good article. It's not about *me*, but it's a good article." He liked the piece, but it was somewhat overdrawn, made more dramatic than his life really was. It portrayed him, Carey felt, to be ferocious, which he wasn't, at least not all the time. Dara Torres had much the same response when Neff wrote about her in *Sports Illustrated*: She liked the article but felt that he somehow overdid the part about how rich she was, that it really wasn't about her, and that it made her sound spoiled. (Some other Mission swimmers found the article too *positive*, portraying her as more dedicated than she, in their view, was.) The problem seemed always to be that the insiders couldn't tell all the real stories, and the outsiders could never know them.

At Nationals, one could see the beginnings of a minor panic as the national reporters assigned to cover swimming at the Olympics began to realize that they didn't know the big names, much less the rising stars; one day the *New York Times* reporter spent a good deal of time running around the deck during the warm-up session, trailed by a photographer, trying to find Mary T. Meagher and some other "stars." Just from sitting up in the stands in the press section, one's sense of the sport changed. The very construction of the building, the steeply sloped spectator seating, effectively blocked one's view of much of the action. A railing separated the first row of seats from the pool deck some ten feet below, and most of the activity in the deck area below that railing—the coaches and athletes talking, swimmers loosening up before a race or brooding after a loss—was invisible to people in the stands. Sitting high up in the bleachers, one could look down only on the swimming pool itself, the lanes clearly laid out. Only the official action (the races themselves) and the official players (eight swimmers in the water and a handful of judges beside it) were visible.

In the summer most of the spectators would be even farther away than that, and would see the Trials and the Olympics only in photographs or on television. The photographers would be looking for interesting shots—color and form and symbol. The results would usually be clichéd: the close finish, the wave from the victory stand, a finger raised for "Number One." At best, a photo could capture the motion of swimming in a blurred time exposure, or the tension of competition in a fisheye view of the ready room, or the pain of dashed hopes in a portrait of a swimmer lying with eyes closed on a bench after a tough loss, but most such things would never be seen by the public.

Because of this distance from the action, the spectators' view of things would be vastly simplified, and only the clearest images would stand out. From a hundred or more feet away, swimmers wearing nylon skin suits all look alike to most people. At Nationals only athletes of almost theatrical proportions stood out from the rest: There was Steve Lundquist, with a huge torso, a thick wave of blond hair, and beautiful teeth that were visible from across the pool—"All-American," they called him. There was Rowdy Gaines, less physically distinctive than Lundquist but charming to reporters and fans alike; with a receding hairline and the hint of a bald patch, he was noticeably the older man in his events, itself a mark of distinction. The crowd could perhaps pick him out. And then there was the anonymous mass, relatively few obvious ethnics like Tony Corbisiero, and no blacks, Chris Silva from UCLA being a noteworthy exception. This was a relatively homogeneous group: white teeth, smooth muscles, clear complexions. And the press focused on these attributes, to show an idealized version of the good swimmer.

In all these cases—and in others, like that of Rick Carey, "the John McEnroe of American swimming," a kind of fabulous athlete-cum-bad boy—the individuals who really lived and swam were transformed into abstract images, concepts almost. Tracy Caulkins became the vulnerable heroine, the best we could offer against the East Germans; she was utterly devoted to her sport, betrayed by the 1980 boycott. Steve Lundquist—who worked part time as a Calvin Klein model, and who was a great interview subject with his candid remarks about whom he liked and didn't, what he thought about partying, and so on—was portrayed as the playboy athlete, the Georgia boy who loved to go fast. The very names of the stars became objects of awe: Mary T. Meagher was "T." to her friends, "Mary

T." to others in the sport, but "Madame Butterfly" to many reporters, though no one in swimming called her that. And name-dropping became a sport among the nonstars. "I talked with *Tracy Caulkins*," a lesser-known swimmer might say. *Swimming World* called her "T.C." with a casual familiarity. Coaches would often call Caulkins, Lundquist, Gaines, or Meagher by their first names, without benefit of introduction.

Some athletes began to make conscious little modifications in their appearance, the better to fit the idealized image the press seemed to require. Meagher had the grace and intelligence to be a media star, but she also had the broad shoulders that betrayed her sport, and so for the benefit of an America that liked its women a bit narrower, she knew how to turn herself at an angle to the camera when photographed to appear less physically dominating. Tiffany Cohen would soften her strong jawline for photographs: for *Interview* magazine by wrapping her lower face in a towel in a mock-seductive pose; for *People* magazine by peering over the edge of the pool, up from the water, so that only her forehead and attractive blue eyes showed in the picture.

The U.S.S. establishment and the press generated official stories, little dramas, a legendary history of American swimming. There were the ritual battles: Could the American women, led by Caulkins and Meagher, defeat the East Germans? Would Rowdy Gaines put aside his doubts and keep swimming? Could Steve Lundquist date beautiful women and still perform in the big meets? There were official histories, which would be repeated in brief during the dull moments of the ABC Olympic coverage: the disaster in Belgrade in 1973, when the East Germans first appeared; the World Championships of 1978, when the American women, led by Caulkins, "served notice to the East Germans and the rest of the world that we were back"; the tragedy of the 1980 boycott. The entire modern history of the sport could and would be packaged into about five sentences, easily understood, with a handful of heroes and heroines.

In this world, new figures would emerge as types: another fourteen-year-old girl challenging the older established stars ("What a pixie, Jim!"), or an older male coming off a major injury ("A courageous comeback, Keith!"). A lore would even develop around training practices: the pain of workouts, the misery of 5:00 A.M. practices before school. Much of the mythology would indeed be created by the swimmers themselves, and the press, the official storytellers and historians, would merely refine and simplify those images. In this way, the reality of these people who like to swim would become transformed into exaggerated talk of dedication and struggle, courage and fear, romance and tragedy.

The new publicity would change the sport, as it always had in Olympic years, by holding up a few select people as somehow utterly different from everyone else, as special. Those few, singled out by the press, would get the attention, and the others would be forgotten. There would be a new factor introduced into swimming in this Olympic year, an inconsistency between one's performance in the pool and one's prestige on the deck. Usually, prestige in swimming reflected how fast one swam, but now it would reflect other, less tangible values and would be awarded at the whim of people who knew almost nothing about the sport. It would become unfair, in a way that many swimmers, some of them members of the Olympic team, would resent deeply; it violated the very heart of the sport, its unambiguous honesty.

The influx of money and publicity could even affect how swimmers performed in competition. One evening at dinner, Mary T. Meagher and Dara Torres were talking about this, complaining about the way the television coverage would hurt their swimming. How carefully one did the warmdown after a race—a few hundred yards of easy swimming to loosen the muscles and clear lactic acid from the bloodstream—could affect one's next race. But the TV people wanted interviews right then, on the spot, right after the event. Meagher vowed then that while she put up with it here at Nationals, during the Olympic Trials the interviews would have to wait. Publicity was nice, especially when coming from the television networks, but finally making a real Olympic team would be better, much better.

Altered Images

The Olympic Trials

ON TUESDAY, MAY 8, 1984, IN A TERSE MEMORANDUM TO the International Olympic Committee, the U.S.S.R. declared that its athletes would not be attending the Los Angeles Olympic Games. Within days, six Soviet allies—East Germany, Bulgaria, Czechoslovakia, Laos, Mongolia, and Vietnam—had followed Moscow's lead. The official explanation was that the United States could not guarantee the safety of the Warsaw Pact athletes. Realistically, more was involved: retaliation for the United States-led boycott of the 1980 Moscow Olympics, for the deployment of U.S. missiles in Western Europe, for President Reagan's rhetorical attacks on the U.S.S.R. (for example, as "the focus of evil in the modern world").

The boycott would decimate the ranks of top competitors in women's swimming at the Games. There would be no Birgit Meineke, the fastest hundred-meter freestyle

swimmer in the world, no Kristin Otto, the fastest swimmer in the two hundred, no Astrid Strauss, who would
have been Tiffany Cohen's main competition in the distance events. Neither Ute Geweniger nor Kathleen Nord
now could challenge Tracy Caulkins in the medleys; the
Russian women could not repeat their 1980 sweep of the
breaststroke events. In television interviews, American
women expressed disappointment that "the best competition wouldn't be there." They knew that the East Germans'
absence improved their own chances for winning events,
but at the same time it lessened the value of those potential
victories. So it was no wonder that their statements to the
press always seemed somehow ambivalent.

A day after the boycott announcement, Mark Schubert
called a team meeting at Mission Viejo. Each of the coaches
said a few words. Schubert then asked if the swimmers
wanted to say anything. Rich Saeger, who had a chance of
making the Olympic team in the two-hundred freestyle and
an even better chance of making the four-by-two-hundred
relay (since four swimmers were chosen, plus two alternates), spoke up.

"None of this is going to make it any easier to make the
American team," he said. There was a pause. He was right.
The Trials had a reputation for being the toughest meet in
American swimming, emotionally. It was a terribly competitive meet, since everyone knew that there were, in
effect, two winners, two swimmers to make the team. That
meant that many swimmers in events with a dominant figure knew that they, too, could be a winner for a day, and
they would all go for it here. In addition, the common rhetoric about "making the team" was really true, it was the
most important thing in the Olympics to all but a very few;
and even those few stars had to make the team before any
gold medals could be won.

Then Saeger said, "Let's go train." Another pause, and

the entire team stood, picked up their gear, and headed out to the pool. That was the end of the meeting.

The 1984 Olympic Trials were held in Indianapolis, at the same fifty-meter pool where spring Nationals had been. The Mission Viejo team stayed at the same Hyatt Hotel. For the preceding three weeks they had done only light work: sharpening up starts and turns, fine-tuning of stroke technique, a last few days of sprinting. The heavy workouts had been cut down so the swimmers could have time to rest, so their bodies could bounce back, stronger than ever, from the work load. This was the "taper." In swimming, the heavy work is done in the months before a big meet; for the last few weeks, the work load is reduced. All the energy that is normally burned off in daily training now accumulates in preparation for a big burst. The physiological peak would be matched by a psychological one: This meet was the Olympic Trials, the only chance in four years for reaching the biggest of all goals in the sport. The toughest competition would be there; everyone was tapered and shaved. The public was (for once) really watching, and no excuses mattered. Now with the work done, and under orders from Schubert to "rest lots," all that the swimmers could do for the next few days was wait.

That would be the worst part. Time and again during the days ahead, the swimmers would say, "I wish I could swim right now." Every young hopeful in the top ranks of swimming would be there, over four hundred in all, tapered and ready to challenge the old veterans like Meagher and Tiffany Cohen and Rowdy Gaines. Even the biggest stars had to point for this meet. Making the team would be as tough as winning a medal at the Games (and in some cases tougher, since only two people "placed" in the Trials), especially with the East Germans staying home.

In Indianapolis, the tension showed. At a press luncheon, Rick Carey, the world record holder in the backstroke, ate two bites and let the rest of his meal grow cold on the plate. At dinner, some just picked at their food. At every meal, whatever the time, there would be outbursts of hysterical giggling, joking, and throwing little bits of food. One evening Dave Barnes, Flo Barker, and Channon Hermstad played with a bunch of grapes from a buffet table: Dave Barnes would put a grape in his mouth and spit it across to the next person, Flo Barker; then Barker would turn and spit the grape in a high arc over to Hermstad. They would get it that far, on a good round, and then try to make the entire circuit (back to Barnes), but it didn't work. Some swimmers nearby thought it was disgusting, but the three, Hermstad and Barnes and Barker, laughed the whole time and kept it up for fifteen or twenty minutes. Others, like Todd Hickman and Matt McClusky ("the tag team," some called them) spent countless quarters playing video games on the third floor of the Hyatt; they especially liked "Pole Position," a race car game well suited to players with fast-twitch muscle and good hand-eye coordination. The younger girls, the thirteen- and fourteen-year-olds on the team, talked everywhere: at dinner, in the hallways, in the cars, at the pool, on the elevators, everywhere, about horror movies and boyfriends, and haircuts and TV shows, about rock music and about who had tickets to the Scorpions' concert in Indy (and how to get over to it that night without Schubert's finding out). Some of the boys talked about attractive girls and unattractive girls, and what their musical tastes were (harder than Dan Fogelberg, softer than ZZ Top).

The meetings between the better swimmers were a little different, the conversations a bit strained; people kept a little more to themselves. There was a premeet barbeque, a U.S.S. tradition at Nationals and other big meets, but only nine or ten Mission swimmers went; they ate some and came right back, not staying around to visit. The swimmers seemed more careful in general—about what they ate, whom they talked to, what they said. This made sense. In swimming, there are no official "lifetime batting average" or "career points scored" statistics; there are no second chances to become great. For these swimmers, all the work and effort came to focus at this one meet. While certainly there were other important meets, a failure here would signal for many of them (especially the older ones who missed the Games in 1980) the end of their careers. Keith Bell, the psychologist from Texas, saw this and understood it. For these athletes, swimming was their life. They had spent the better part of their twenty or so years working at it, and it mattered to them more than anything else in the world. So the Olympic Trials were, for them, a matter of life—their life and how they had spent it—and death, or at least a terrible failure. Bell knew that in matters of life and death one is finally alone. There was nothing much he could say to them at Trials, or that they could say to each other.

As usual, Schubert was relaxed and confident. While during the regular season he would frown at horseplay, now he laughed at it; things that normally might offend him he now shrugged off. At a team meeting early in the week he reminded the swimmers, referring to the pay channels in the hotel that offered "adult" fare, not to stay up late "watching T&A on TV." The remark got a big laugh, except that some of the younger swimmers didn't understand the joke and had to ask for an explanation. It was, for Schubert, an uncharacteristic comment, a kind of letting his hair down. One evening at dinner, with everyone around laughing and talking, Schubert himself got the giggles, recalling how, in 1979 on a U.S. National team trip to Japan, he had gone into a video game parlor and over a two-day period had spent, as he remembered it, over a hundred dollars playing "Space Invaders."

The Olympic Trials

If Schubert was calm—which he seemed to be, despite the hints of nervous laughter—he had a right to be, for the Mission team had prepared as well for this meet as for any in its history. The training for the past year, since Meagher arrived in September, had been tremendous, with athletes from all around the world motivated as well as they would ever be, working as hard as they could. At the Trials themselves, Mission had, as usual, covered every contingency in feeding, housing, and transporting the swimmers. There were even a few extra staff members, more than at Nationals. One especially stood out: Haik Gharibians, a physiotherapist from Canada, with long experience working with world-class athletes in all sports. Gharibians, a short, round, bald-headed fellow, full of stories and concern, had filled his room down at one end of the hall with over ten thousand dollars' worth of medical equipment donated from all over the United States—whirlpools, ultrasound machines, special tables and pads and electronic devices usable only by the initiated. ("A physiotherapist is not a masseur," he would explain. "A physiotherapist is university-trained; he has a degree.") Gharibians' room, with the swimmers getting rubdowns at all hours of the day, became a social center for the Mission team during Trials. He welcomed everyone. The swimmers would lie on the tables getting rubdowns, watching the color TV, talking with Gharibians or somebody else. The younger girls found him "adorable" and, behind his back, looked at his round shape and called him "Pac-Man." There were the other staff members, too, who handled the rooms and the billing and the transportation, all wearing their yellow or blue or white shirts, freshly laundered, remembering to choose the color according to which day of the meet it was—first blue, then white, then yellow.

On Monday morning, June 25, 1984, Channon Hermstad was to swim the four-hundred-meter individual medley. It would be the first big final of the meet for a Mission Viejo swimmer. This event provided her with her best chance for making the Olympic team, and everyone on the team knew it.

A week before, though, while coming down the stairs in her house one night, Hermstad had slipped and sprained her ankle. She had had it taped at practice for the past few days. One day the tape job was poor, and Hermstad had written on the tape, in pen, "Joke," referring to the taping job. She favored that leg, never said anything about it, but limped a little and was swimming badly. In Indianapolis, for the last few days before the Trials started, she still favored the leg and would go in to Haik Gharibians, the physiotherapist, every now and then for heat treatment. It seemed to Gharibians at the time that the injury was distracting her. When asked once about the effect it would have on her swimming, he indicated that perhaps physically the ankle was all right, but . . . he would shake his head. An injury like this was very tough right before a big meet.

Hermstad herself ("Hermie" to her friends—and she had many) never said anything in public, but she thought a lot about the ankle. She never knew when a dive or a turn would aggravate the sprain. On Monday night when she stepped up on the starting block for the four-hundred individual medley she was thinking about the race, and was a little worried, if only unconsciously, about her ankle. The gun fired. She dove into the water and, instead of streamlining out under the surface, she almost immediately popped up, a yard or more behind the rest of the field. It was a terrible start. From there on she was thinking, "What am I doing here? What's wrong with my stroke?" She felt funny, uncomfortable, in the water; and she was *thinking* the entire time. She knew then, and she knew in retrospect, that thinking during a race was a mistake; it seemed to destroy the ease of moving in the water. Swimming fast had to come from instinct and habit, nothing more.

Hermstad's swim was a disaster. When it was finally over, she had finished well back in the pack, with a time of 4:57, almost ten seconds slower than she had swum in winning at Nationals. She wasn't even close to qualifying for the finals that evening. She came back to the bleachers where the Mission team sat, wearing her Mission Viejo blue and gold bathrobe with the hood up, crying quietly, and stood facing the pool. Her friend Dave Barnes talked to her a bit, and he hugged her for a long time. Mary T. Meagher stood behind her, rubbing her neck. The three of them watched in silence as the preliminaries began for the men's two-hundred freestyle.

Meagher, herself very bright and thoughtful, knew that Hermstad's own analysis was correct: You can't think too much about what you're doing. One night at dinner Meagher sat and explained to a visitor that to swim fast in a big meet you just had to dive in and let all your cares go: "No brain—no pain," was the way she put it. Meagher always applied that principle in her big races. She would simply disengage her critical faculties, her mind, forget all the worrying and the anxiety and let instinct and her body take over. If the preparation has been right, if the stroke techniques have become second nature and the physiology has been properly conditioned, then everything will fall into place.

Other great swimmers knew it, too, if only instinctively. One night, before the finals of the women's two-hundred free, the eight women who would compete for the Olympic berths were waiting in the glass-walled Ready Room to be called up. Carrie Steinseifer, who had already made the team in the hundred free, lay on the floor; so did Mary T. herself, waving her legs back and forth—this was not one of her best events. Marybeth Linzmeier, a veteran of the

1980 Trials (and this her best event), leaned against the wall with her eyes closed; so did Sippy Woodhead, her head covered by the hood of her sweat shirt, lost in herself. And then there was Mary Wayte—an eighteen-year-old youngster (compared to the survivors of 1980) from Washington State. Someone in the room had a Sony radio on, playing a Commodores song called "Brick House." Wayte sang along a little, and when the singer said "36-24-36," Wayte kidded, "I should be a brick house," and a few of the women laughed, but most (including Sippy Woodhead) were in there sweating their hearts out, waiting for what could be the biggest race of their lives. But Mary Wayte was walking around the room, laughing and telling jokes. Later she remembered the small talk ("It was dumb"), that the conversation involved "nothing that required thinking," and, especially, that no one could shake Sippy out of her concentration.

Wayte went on to take second (as good as winning, at the Trials) in that event, four one-hundredths of a second behind Woodhead. Four weeks later, a few minutes before the Olympic Finals in the two-hundred freestyle, Mary Wayte would go over to Woodhead, her strongest competition, smile and say "Good luck," and give Sippy a big bear hug. Some people sitting in the stands watching them would think, God, that's the end of Woodhead, the brooding veteran, regarded as a "head case" like no other; this young be-bopper comes by and says "Good luck" and gives her a hug at a time like this. (Mary Wayte went on to win the Olympic finals, the gold medal, and after the race she would congratulate Woodhead yet again.)

Like Meagher, Wayte could just let things go. In an almost unbearably stressful situation, she seemed not to worry. The very best of them were like that. "No brain—no pain."

*   *   *

Coming into the Olympic Trials, Mary T. Meagher held the world records in both the hundred- and two-hundred-meter butterfly. Both had been set in the Walter Schroeder Natatorium in Brown Deer, Wisconsin, just outside Milwaukee, in August 1981. The times bordered on the incredible: 57.93 in the hundred (and no one, Meagher included, had ever swum a hundred fly in the fifty-eight-second span) and 2:05.96 in the two hundred. Meagher herself, easing off from hard training during her years at Cal, had not approached these times in the four years since. But for the past year, since joining the Mission Viejo team, she had trained very hard, and was trying to beat them in the Olympics. Mark Schubert knew that she was thinking about those records; but he also thought that perhaps her 1981 swims were like Bob Beamon's broad jump in Mexico City in 1968—performances years ahead of their time, stunning, miraculous almost; if they were never again approached, it was no shame to the athlete.

Meagher was now in good form. Even Tracy Caulkins, who had at one time held the American record in the two-hundred fly, avoided swimming against her. When planning how to win the most gold medals at Los Angeles Caulkins chose to train for the backstroke events rather than butterfly, knowing that, while it would be easier to make the team in the butterfly, her chance of actually beating Meagher for the gold medal was very slim indeed.

Most of Meagher's ten siblings and both parents came up from Louisville to Indianapolis for the Trials, wearing shirts that said on the front, "This is a Mary T-shirt" and sporting straw skimmers with red, white, and blue bands around them. They waved flags, handed out bumper stickers ("$H^2O + T = Au$"), waved to the TV cameras, and in general were the most visible, vocal, and well-organized cheering section at the Trials, filling an entire seating area of the IUPUI swim stadium. Meagher herself needed the support; the boycott bothered her, since she knew that there would forever be speculation about "what if the East Germans had come."

The hundred-meter butterfly would be swum on Thursday, and the two-hundred on Saturday, the last day of the meet. In the Thursday morning preliminary heats of the hundred, Jenna Johnson of Industry Hills, California, qualified first in just over fifty-nine seconds. Meagher finished second, her time just over a minute. It was the first time that year that Meagher had failed to go under a minute in the hundred at a major meet.

Her competition was tough, too. Jenna Johnson was young, only sixteen years old, but stood over six feet tall and was stunningly fast in the sprints. She had a good shot at making the Olympic team in both the hundred fly and the hundred-meter freestyle, where with each stroke her long arms could take her farther than any other swimmer in the race. She had very fast reactions to the starting gun and was strong. In both the fly and the free she would, from the start, jump out to a big lead, take the turn at the far end of the fifty-meter pool, then—her lack of endurance being her great weakness—try to hang on for the second lap of the two-lap race. Despite the fact that the younger woman was relatively new to the national swimming scene, Meagher had paid attention to her career and knew about Johnson's racing style.

So in the finals of the hundred fly, when Johnson went out fast, clearly ahead, Meagher wasn't surprised. About three quarters of the way down the pool on the first lap Meagher glanced over and saw Johnson out in front; they turned well ahead of the pack, and coming back, Meagher began to come on, she thought at the time not fast, but as she later saw the ABC videotape playbacks, it was indeed fast. She could come on very quickly near the end of the race as Johnson (and most others) would begin to sink lower in the water. Meagher, as always, would continue to ride high, with her hips up. Meagher indeed came on, but Johnson's lead was too much. Meagher took second, which in the Olympic Trials was as good as first. Still, it was a frustrating loss. She had made the Olympic team, but people said her stroke looked bad, and the boycott was nagging at her. Coaches on the deck were used to seeing her as the most superb flyer in the sport. Afterward, the ABC commentators tried to analyze the race and show what was "wrong" with Meagher's stroke, and ask why she wasn't swimming "fast." But Meagher was basically satisfied. She had made the team.

In the two hundred no one was even close to her. In the prelims she finished first by three seconds. In the finals that evening she was out at the halfway mark two seconds ahead of second-place Nancy Hogshead. At the finish it was Meagher in 2:07.53, then Hogshead second at 2:11.25, making the team in her third individual event.

Again, Meagher was not completely happy with her performance. She had felt okay in the hundred—not great, though—and so wasn't expecting anything special. Even so, she hoped that a month later in Los Angeles she would go faster in the new Olympic pool with the crowds and the excitement of the Games. She didn't plan to do any more hard training. Over the past year, working out at Mission Viejo, she had swum more yards and harder sets than ever before in her career. She had lost that excess weight from college and knew she was ready to swim a good two-hundred fly.

Mike O'Brien's parents and grandparents came to Indianapolis for the Trials, but they stayed out of Mike's way. They didn't take rooms at the Hyatt, where the Mission Viejo team stayed. Schubert insisted on having no parents around, and Mr. and Mrs. O'Brien knew that the policy was a good one. Mrs. O'Brien knew that she would have trouble sleeping during the Trials, and Mike didn't need any more distractions than he would have already. He had four events—four chances to make the Olympic team.

He swam the two-hundred free the first day, just after Channon Hermstad's disastrous four-hundred IM. It was his shortest event, a sprint really; and while he hadn't expected to make the team in it, he wanted to do well. The time—1:51—was a good one for him, his best by one and a half seconds, but not fast enough to make the team. Over the next few days he failed to qualify for the team in the four-hundred IM, and then in the four-hundred free, his second-best event, where he finished third. The competition was very tough. O'Brien was swimming well, very well; his speed was noticeably better, and together with his usual endurance this meant that his chances were good. But other people were also doing well.

By Saturday he had only one chance left, the fifteen-hundred-meter freestyle. In the preliminaries of the fifteen hundred, held the day before, O'Brien had qualified second to George DiCarlo. Saturday evening's final would be the big race.

O'Brien and his friend Scott Brackett went over to the pool to warm up during the preliminaries. After the morning prelims were over, they climbed into the big LTD station wagon that Ris Pyykko, husband of Schubert's secretary, was driving to shuttle swimmers between the Hyatt and the pool, and headed back for some lunch and rest before the big race. O'Brien was in the front seat, on the passenger side; Brackett was in back. Two blocks from the hotel, as they were heading through a green light, a blue Toyota Celica cut across three lanes of traffic from their right and turned left in front of them. Pyykko slammed on the brakes. The station wagon slid perhaps seventy feet and crashed into the side of the Celica, just in front of the driver's seat. O'Brien's knees hit the dashboard; his head bumped the windshield, though not hard; Pyykko and Brackett were shaken. Pyykko took a minute to catch his breath and asked if everyone in the car was okay. All said yes. They climbed out of the station wagon and surveyed the damage. Pyykko, all too aware that the swimmers might have been injured in some hidden way, and knowing, too, that both of them had qualified to swim in the final that evening, told O'Brien and Brackett to leave now, before the police arrived, and go on back to the hotel. They walked the two blocks remaining back to the hotel, leaving Pyykko to handle whatever problems might arise. Upon arriving at the Hyatt, O'Brien immediately went up to see Haik Gharibians, the physiotherapist, who iced the knee and noted that the injuries were minor. When Mark Schubert heard about the accident he wondered if years of hard work were going down the drain.

O'Brien tried to shake off the accident and focus on his race plan for that evening. Earlier in the week, George Di-Carlo had established himself as the favorite in the distance event by breaking Brian Goodell's American four-hundred-free record, the second-oldest standard on the books, set seven years before. DiCarlo had gone out fast in that swim, but O'Brien had come on near the end, nearly taking the gold, only to be touched out by both DiCarlo and John Mykkanen. After that race, O'Brien's strategy revolved around overcoming DiCarlo's early speed. For over a year now O'Brien had worked to become more aggressive, to challenge the leaders early, then put them away in the later stages of the race with his long strokes and powerful endurance. So his plan was fairly simple: Go out strong from the beginning and continually increase the pressure throughout the race.

DiCarlo and O'Brien, the top two qualifiers, would

swim in lanes four and five, in the center of the pool. The race would be for fifteen hundred meters, thirty lengths of the pool.

From the gun, DiCarlo surged to the front, followed closely by Chris Hansen of Arden Hills and Matt Cetlinski of Holmes Lumber, the University of Florida's club. The pack, save DiCarlo, was closely bunched, with O'Brien and his friend Scott Brackett at the rear.

By the three-hundred-meter mark, O'Brien, pressing hard, had moved up to third behind DiCarlo and Hansen; the others were close behind.

By the four hundred, DiCarlo led the pack by more than two full seconds, and O'Brien was moving out toward him, leaving the others. Hansen was quickly fading, exhausted after his early sprint; the rest of the field seemed to be finding their own speed, unable to maintain the brutal pace that DiCarlo, who was obviously going after a record, was setting. At some time during these early laps, O'Brien's goggles fogged over, so he could not see the signals Mark Schubert was trying to make from the deck; so he had no idea how fast they were moving, although he did realize that the pace was demanding. He just decided to hang with DiCarlo.

DiCarlo was swimming straight down the middle of his lane, staying in the smoothest water. This allowed O'Brien, using a standard technique for well-taught swimmers, to move over close to the lane line alongside DiCarlo and "drag off of him"—in effect, riding along on the faster swimmer's wake. In a sprint, the swimmer can gain considerable speed with this method, more or less body-surfing at the expense of the leaders. In the distance races, the effect is less noticeable to the spectator, but important nonetheless. At the seven hundred, however, DiCarlo shifted away to the far side of his lane, leaving his own best water in order to cut O'Brien out of a free ride. In effect, DiCarlo had recognized that this was now a two-man race. In the next hundred meters he gained two tenths of a second, a small but noticeable distance, certainly helpful in the Olympic Trials.

Still O'Brien held on. He knew, despite the blindness caused by the fogged goggles, that DiCarlo was setting a very fast pace; he knew now that the race was between the two of them; and, finally, he knew that if he stayed with DiCarlo and finished second he would win a spot on the Olympic team.

At eleven hundred meters—with only four hundred to go—DiCarlo heard the crowd roaring and knew that he must be ahead of Goodell's American record pace. At that moment O'Brien made a move to catch him, digging down into his last reserves. But DiCarlo was too tough, and O'Brien's strength had reached its limits, drained by the pressure of staying close during the early laps.

When it finally was over, DiCarlo had indeed broken the American record for the fifteen-hundred-meter free-style; O'Brien finished three seconds behind him, dropping his own personal best time nearly ten seconds. The rest of the field came in gradually, strung out behind. Despite the automobile accident earlier in the day and a pair of sore knees, Mike O'Brien had made the U.S. Olympic team.

If his luck was good, Rowdy Gaines' swimming career would be over in another month and a half. If his luck was bad, it would end in three days. Gaines came into the Olympic Trials favored to win both the hundred- and the two-hundred-meter freestyles, but everyone (Gaines most of all) knew that at Trials a pack of young kids would come out, unknowns with nothing to lose who could take their races out hard, and through a miracle of adrenaline hang on to gain a spot on the team; and they would all be gunning for Rowdy Gaines. On his side, Gaines had a history of tough NCAA championships, international competitions, and world-record swims. He had more accumulated top-level swimming experience than any but a few close rivals. If he were in good form, he should be able to make the hundred and maybe the two hundred. In any case he should place in the top four in both, thus making the two freestyle relays.

Like Meagher, Gaines had been at the top of the sport for five years now, belying the myth that swimmers' careers are short and intense. He had been in swimming long enough, and with enough successes, that here at Indianapolis he was a genuine celebrity. Teenage girls in midriff-baring tops approached him with pens and programs for autographs. Some with cameras wanted pictures of Rowdy talking with Mark Spitz, or of Rowdy with Dara Torres, or of Rowdy with one of the girls themselves, giggling and blushing, alternately pulling close to him then turning away, laughing, while a friend snapped the picture. Only a few other swimmers—Tracy Caulkins, Steve Lundquist, Mary T. Meagher—got this kind of attention.

But Gaines wasn't thinking about the groupies. He was thinking about his races and what would follow them. He had mentally rehearsed—before the first race, before the meet even—how he would come to the press after losing and tell them it had been an honor just to compete in the Olympic Trials and how great the new young swimmers like Heath were. He had found himself thinking about losing, almost preparing to lose races, and that was bad.

On Monday, the first day of the meet, he qualified second in the two hundred. Mike Heath from the University of Florida led the qualifiers with a new American record, breaking Gaines' old standard. Five swimmers were under 1:50 in the preliminaries, all five swimming fast enough to have taken the silver medal at the Moscow Olympic Games. In the finals that night, Gaines went out fast, very fast. At the 150, three quarters of the way through the race, he was out front, on a pace fast enough to break the world record. But over the last twenty or twenty-five meters he died, as Mike Heath, then Jeff Float, David Larson, and Bruce Hayes went by; and then Geoff Gaberino and Rich Saeger. By the time they reached the wall, Rowdy Gaines was in seventh place, failing not only to make the team in the two hundred, but even to make the team for the four-by-two-hundred relay. He didn't even qualify for one of the two *alternate* positions for the relay.

"That was the stupidest race I ever swam," he said afterward. "There was just no reason for it." "How bad did I feel?" he responded to the *Los Angeles Times* reporter. "Well, let's put it this way. I opened the curtains and looked out the window from my hotel room on the eleventh floor. Then I said, 'Well, let's think about this.'"

After the disastrous two hundred he realized that maybe he had panicked, had thought so much about losing that he had forgotten how to win. But then the widespread support for him in swimming came out as over the next two days countless swimmers and coaches—some of whom coached opposing swimmers—wished him luck in the hundred, to be swum on Wednesday night. His family talked with him. Even Mark Spitz, who was covering the Trials for ABC, talked with him. One morning he had breakfast with Tiffany Cohen, who was disappointed with her own early races, although she would go on easily to make the team in the four hundred and eight hundred. Cohen told him that when she wasn't swimming well, she tried to get angry with herself, get mad about how she was doing, and that helped her get tough.

But Gaines was less angry with himself than just scared—not so much of the other swimmers as of himself. He was afraid of losing the big race. He *hated* losing. This week, at this meet, he was physically ready to win, he

knew that; but then so was Mike Heath and almost everyone else. The real competition in the hundred would be
mental. The race would be to see who would crack under
the pressure and who would hold up.

On Wednesday morning he qualified first in the hundred free in 49.99 seconds. Between Gaines and Geoff
Gaberino of Florida, who qualified eighth, there was less
than nine tenths of a second. The hundred free final that
evening would be anybody's race. Gaines would swim in
lane four, in the middle of the pool, next to Mike Heath,
winner of the two-hundred free, who had qualified second.

It seemed to last only an instant. When it was all over,
Heath had won in 49.87, and Gaines took second in 49.96.
Gaines had made the team and would swim both the hundred free and the free relay in Los Angeles. They stood on
the victory stand, Heath and Gaines, and when Gaines' second-place finish was announced, the crowd in the IUPUI
stands roared their approval, and some people on the deck
cried. After the ABC interview, Gaines and Heath stood together and watched the videotape replay of the race several
times. Gaines called Heath "the next great American
sprinter" and said that today at Indianapolis, getting second was as good as winning. But in thirty more days it
wouldn't be as good as winning; and certainly, as he
looked ahead, he didn't plan to take second in that, the
final swimming meet of his career.

Dara Torres had to swim the first event of the Olympic
Trials on the first day of the meet, the women's hundred-
meter freestyle. Even if she finished in the top four and
made the team in a relay position, the pressure wouldn't be
entirely off until the last day of the meet because of relay
challenges. At any time, a swimmer who had not entered
an individual event from which relays were picked (such
as the hundred free, from which the four-by-hundred relay

team was chosen) could challenge for a relay spot, swimming an individual time trial at the end of the day's events. Tracy Caulkins, with the possibility of six or seven gold medals, probably would do just that, trying to bump someone from the relay. But on Monday, June 25, Dara Torres needed to make the team and had to finish in the top four.

For the past year at Mission this had been her goal. Over her bed at home was a sign: "26.4 + 28.4 = 54.8"— her ideal splits to tie the world record (or almost; the record was 54.79, set by the D.D.R.'s Barbara Krause). For two years she had been the fastest fifty-meter swimmer in the world, but the second lap of the hundred continued to be her downfall, despite the fact that the training at Mission had improved her endurance. She came into the Olympic Trials seeded third, with a 56.54.

She qualified third for the finals, behind Carrie Steinseifer and Jenna Johnson. At the finals that evening, after the Decatur Central High School Jazz Band had finished its routine, the pool was cleared, and the first final, the women's hundred-meter freestyle, was called to the blocks. Torres came to the blocks with her fingernails painted blue with yellow lettering showing her goal time: 54.8. If she did it, she would tie the world record.

The race was short and fast, ending less than a minute after it began. Dara Torres finished fourth, behind Hogshead, Steinseifer, and Johnson. Torres had made the Olympic Team and would swim on the free relay—a solid bet for a gold medal and maybe a world record. But she would not swim the individual hundred freestyle. After the race she swam a few easy widths of the diving well. She stopped at one point to hang on the wall by herself, crying.

On the last night of the Trials, Tracy Caulkins decided to swim a challenge time trial for a spot on the free relay. If Caulkins' time were faster than Torres', Torres would be dropped to an alternate spot, thus missing any chance for a gold medal. When Caulkins got up for the individual time trial in the swim stadium, Dara Torres put on her Sony Walkman, turned up the volume so high that several by-standers could hear the music, and ran into the women's locker room behind the stands. As Caulkins dove in and started her swim, Torres stood inside the locker room door, talking loudly and singing and moaning to herself, "Oh, God," over and over. For a moment a friend was with her, but Torres didn't know it; and even if she had known it, it wouldn't have mattered, for she felt very alone as she slumped down to sit in a corner of the locker room, hold-ing her legs.

When it was over, Caulkins did not beat Torres' time, did not even come close. Dara Torres would go to the Olympic Games.

In all, six swimmers from Mission Viejo made the U.S. Olympic swimming team: Dara Torres, Mike O'Brien, Mary T. Meagher, Tiffany Cohen (who won both the four-hun-dred and eight-hundred freestyles in the Trials), Amy White, and Rich Saeger, who would be an alternate for the four-by-two-hundred relay. So did Rowdy Gaines of Winter Haven, Florida, swimming for Longhorn Aquatics of Aus-tin, Texas, along with fifteen other 1980 Olympians, and Jill Sterkel, the 1980 and 1976 Olympian. Of the forty-three swimmers chosen for the Olympic team, seventeen were from California. Mark Schubert was selected as one of the nine Olympic staff coaches.

Four American record holders failed to place in the top two in any event and so didn't make the Olympic team. Two of those, Bill Barrett and Craig Beardsley, had been captains of U.S. National teams and had held world rec-ords within the past year. In her last chance to make the team, 1983 Pan American champion Sue Walsh finished third in the hundred-meter backstroke and spent forty minutes after the race sitting on a bench next to the diving pool, holding her head in her hands.

For years these swimmers had done things that many of their contemporaries—and probably most people in America—found silly, or ridiculous, or even "sick": those morning workouts, swimming four and a half hours a day, lifting weights an hour a day besides, traveling across the United States to swim just one event in a very fast meet, skipping school for a week at a time to go to Nationals. They wore the thinnest, tightest suits the rules would allow; they shaved their bodies; some wore ski gloves before races to keep their hands warm, in hopes that the little extra blood circulation would give them a better "feel" for the water. There was no room for being "cool," for staying even a little bit detached.

And as Schubert had told his swimmers before the Trials, "No excuse in the world counts for squat." Channon Hermstad sprained an ankle at the Trials—but Mike O'Brien was in a car accident. Jeanne Childs' stroke was off—but Mary T. Meagher's was not at its best, either. They came into this meet having tried their hardest, yet aware that it may not have been enough. They came in, the best of them, with no excuses.

That commitment produces one great advantage. When the day of competition comes, one can fairly say: *No one has worked so hard or sacrificed so much as I have. Every day when it was possible to work out, I was working out. I watched my diet, went to bed on time, did the proper warm-up, wore the proper suit, checked my goggles twice. I moved away from home at thirteen, lifted weights until my muscles collapsed, even skipped my high-school graduation so I wouldn't miss a workout. Every day I have practiced committing myself to this sport. And now I am going to give everything I have to this race. By God, I deserve to win.*

The Olympic Trials offered them one chance, the chance of a lifetime. Before each event, on the parade up to the starting blocks, the finalists would pass by the stands with their eyes glazed over, looking vaguely toward the pool, lost to everyone but themselves. Minutes later, when the races were over, the losers sat or stood; on their faces were easy tears and painful smiles; and if you went over and spoke to one of them, Joan Pennington, or Bill Barrett, or Jeanne Childs, it seemed they couldn't really hear what you were saying.

On Saturday night, at the end of the week, the forty-three swimmers who made the U.S. Olympic team were each presented with a rose and a Certificate of Achievement and were made Honorary Citizens of Indianapolis, Indiana.

10

The Olympic Games

THE OLYMPIC GAMES ARE, ABOVE ALL, A PUBLIC EVENT. IN the Olympics, fame comes quickly; apart from the Olympics, a swimmer finds it difficult to achieve any fame at all. A swimmer like Craig Beardsley can dominate his event, be captain of the U.S. National team, win national and world titles, hold world records for years and years—and never be known outside of the swimming community itself. But an unknown young swimmer can, with a single great season encompassing the Trials and Games, win an Olympic gold and go down in the record book and public memory. At Nationals one achieves the adulation of the rest of the swimming community, but only the Olympics can make one famous, can set up roles in the movies, can open the chance to parlay gold medals into a lifetime career.

The Olympics are different in other ways as well. For most swimmers, they come only once or twice in a career.

Tracy Caulkins in her career would swim in nineteen National championships, but she swam in only one Olympics. Then, too, the Olympics are special in their emphasis on winning. A fast time, so central to the sport at all other meets, becomes irrelevant here, as the gold medal becomes the standard. Times will fall, but the gold medal remains.

By the end of the Trials in June 1984, the press had already zeroed in on the potential heroes of the U.S. swimming team, chosen for a combination of their talent, looks, charm, and willingness to give good interviews to reporters. Rowdy Gaines was given the chance; so was the big blond breaststroker Steve Lundquist; so, too, Tracy Caulkins, at that time probably the best all-around swimmer in America; and so with Mary T. Meagher. There were a few others, perhaps, but beyond these, most of the swimmers who made the Olympic team (even some who would win gold medals) were to remain completely anonymous to the vast American public.

If the Trials irrevocably divided those who didn't make the Olympic team from those who did, the training camp (somewhat less dramatically) divided those who just made the team from the true stars. At the Trials, Gaines and Lundquist dominated the news with their outgoing, attractive style, while less glamorous types such as Mike Heath—who had beaten Gaines in both the hundred and two-hundred at Trials—received relatively little attention. Some swimmers resented the attention given Gaines and Lundquist. Several of them even talked of how Gaines seemed to play with the press with his "maybe I will, maybe I won't" routine; his crying after the two-hundred free at the Pan Ams; the attention he got from some of the younger, especially female, members of the U.S. team there, as if he encouraged their pleas of "Oh, Rowdy, keep swimming for us." Some of his Olympic teammates saw him as more than a little cocky, too sure of himself, and an inconsistent worker at best. At least one top coach pri-

vately called him a crybaby and a wimp. And Steve Lundquist, the breaststroke swimmer, was in fact one of the
hardest-working swimmers in America, incredibly competitive, a man who drove himself to win everything he swam,
in every practice, from the warm-up right on through the
final sprints. But he had a press image as a hard-drinking,
womanizing young stud, a late-night playboy who'd show
up at the last minute and win it all for the U.S.A. Some
coaches and swimmers were bothered by this image and
found it not only misleading—for many of them deeply respected Lundquist's work habits and intensity in the
sport—but also bad for swimming's public image.

The separation of stars and unknowns was obvious
from the first day of the Olympic training camp in Mission
Viejo. The athletes had flown from Indianapolis, settled in
their rooms on the fourth floor of the Holiday Inn at
Laguna Hills, just across the freeway from Mission Viejo,
and begun the four weeks of training leading up to the
Games. On the first day of the camp, U.S.S. held a Media
Day at the Marguerite pool so all the television and newspaper people could come in and talk with the team. For the
younger swimmers, unused to publicity, the event was exciting; for the old, established stars, it was boring. Tracy
Caulkins was nowhere to be seen. Rowdy Gaines showed
up with his hair looking like he'd just stuck his finger in an
electrical socket. Steve Lundquist was strolling around the
deck with a plug of chewing tobacco under his lip. By contrast, young Mike O'Brien was eager to be interviewed.
This was his first taste of publicity.

In the next four weeks, though, O'Brien would have
other things to think about. Ever since he was thirteen
years old, O'Brien had had problems with his left ankle, a
weakness in the ligaments that sometimes gave way to
sprains. In the first week of the training camp, as he
walked down some stairs, O'Brien slipped and twisted his
ankle badly (similar to Channon Hermstad's problem at the

Trials, which destroyed her chances for making the team).
Weak ankles seemed common among top-rank swimmers,
who also generally have very flexible ankles, making it
easier for the kick to be genuinely propulsive. Imagine
swimming freestyle with ankles so stiff that the toes are
pointing straight to the bottom of the pool as you lie on
your stomach; the feet would be practically anchors, slow-
ing the swimmer down. The toes have to be pointing
straight back at least, and good swimmers can in fact let
them flex past the straight line with the rest of the leg. For
the next two weeks of the four in the camp, O'Brien would
rise at 4:00 A.M. and trainer Ted Becker would laboriously
tape the ankle so he could at least get in and swim. But
with his foot locked into a right angle with his leg, he was
swimming very slowly at the end of the line that moved up
and down the pool. The ankle bothered him and interfered
with his training, but O'Brien had tremendous faith in
himself and wasn't going to let an ankle stop him.

Mark Schubert was not so optimistic. While O'Brien
was very tough mentally, still Schubert talked with Olympic Head Coach Don Gambril about taking O'Brien out of
the fifteen hundred and replacing him with Dan Jorgenson,
who had finished third at the Trials. The conversation was
a casual one, just a mention of the possibility, and they
decided not to do it after all, but their concern was real.

There were nine coaches on the Olympic staff. Seven of
them had been chosen before the Trials even took place, so
there was no guarantee that an Olympic coach would have
any swimmers on the team. As it happened, Gambril had
no swimmers on the team (although he had a long history
of placing swimmers, and his position was in part a recognition of that); neither did Frank Keefe, nor did Ray Bus-
sard. During the training camp, Mark Schubert was
responsible for his six swimmers—O'Brien, Meagher,
Torres, Cohen, Saeger, and Amy White. They took the far
lane against the wall in the Marguerite pool—the Animal

Lane—and did their workouts there. The middle lanes of
the pool were occupied by a number of different groups:
coaches with a few swimmers each, generally groups
mixed from several different clubs, and coaches with
swimmers they had not worked with before. In the lane
nearest Marguerite Parkway, on the opposite side from
Schubert's group, were the University of Florida swimmers, coached by Randy Reese.

For years the University of Florida team had been Mission Viejo's nearest rival in American club swimming, and
Reese, their coach, was Schubert's counterpart on the East
Coast. Schubert and Reese were roughly the same age—
mid-thirties—and their coaching styles were somewhat
similar: Both are known as tough, no-nonsense coaches
who demand complete commitment. Both command loy-
alty and obedience. Schubert's success is in the organization of a powerful team; Reese's claim is in creating
national champions out of relative unknowns. Year after
year, his University of Florida team takes good—not always great—high-school swimmers and brings them to the
top of the sport. He brought Mike Heath to the first-place
stand at the Olympic Trials. He also trained Tracy Caulkins
in her college years. In 1983 his team won the NCAA
men's championship without taking a single first-place
event—a tribute to his ability to get the most from every
member of his team with whatever talent is available. Like
Schubert, he speaks quietly to his athletes, but they listen;
unlike Schubert, he occasionally swears. His swimmers are
college students and are more boisterous than the younger
Mission Viejo athletes. According to his swimmers, Reese
is consumed by the sport, thinking about it always, perhaps more than Schubert does. If you go out to dinner with
him, he'll talk about swimming. He's well known for coming up with new training methods, new tricks for building
strength. In the fall, at the beginning of the season, his
swimmers go out to the University of Florida's Gator Sta-

dium and run up and down the stadium seats lifting "heavyhands" weights; then they will rest their knees on homemade trolleys—wheels fastened onto either end of a one-foot board—and roll themselves, using their hands, up the ramps that go to the upper level of the stadium. Their warm-up routine always includes stroke drills, which demand extra concentration. Several times in a workout a trainer may take blood samples from them, testing the level of lactic acid; they do kicking sets with old tennis shoes on. His swimmers thrive on the novelty of his training methods and are proud of the physical demands put on them. They get strong in Reese's program.

Randy Reese is a small, dour man with a trimmed moustache, which with another inch or two of growth would make a nice handlebar. He rarely smiles, and he has a sense of humor so dry it is missed by most listeners. His cold, hard style intimidates reporters, so they tend to shy away from interviewing him and his swimmers. His swimmers know that Reese's bad-guy image does not quite fit the reality. Under the right conditions—when he is not busy working with his athletes—he is easy to talk with, forthright, intelligent, and even, in his own blunt way, cordial.

Schubert, on the other hand, cultivates the press with help from the Mission Viejo Company and the Philip Morris connection. The scenic beauty of Mission Viejo is ideal for press photographers, especially given the added attraction of great divers in the next pool. So other things being equal, Schubert's swimmers are more likely than Reese's to get the press coverage: Reese's team is filled with quiet, often shy—Mike Heath is a prime case—hard-working college men, Schubert's filled with laughing, excitable high-school girls. Schubert, too, cultivated his position *within* U.S. Swimming, his relationship to the top officials and executives in the organization, while Reese seems at best indifferent to some of those officials. At coaches' clinics and conventions, Schubert's sentiments about making the sport fun for younger swimmers appeal to the mass of local-level coaches, who often don't know how different the top ranks really are. When, by contrast, Reese gives talks, the visiting coaches from local teams are sometimes shocked at what he says, his hard language and harder policies ("If a kid comes in to practice with a 'shoulder problem,' I let him kick the whole practice. I've cured a lot of shoulder problems" or "If you've got a fever, you're sick and should go home. If you're just puking, you stay and swim").

Schubert and Reese worked with the largest groups at the Olympic training camp. Richard Quick of Texas was coaching a few swimmers (Rowdy Gaines was one of them), and Charlie Hodgson of Miami had his group. The intensity of these groups was high, but several other coaches seemed almost superfluous for whatever reasons and spent the morning sessions talking among themselves around the coffee pot at the end of the pool. At least one of the better swimmers grew disappointed with his coach and wanted to transfer over to Reese's group, which he saw as more serious, more organized, and more committed. Certainly Reese's reputation among the other swimmers was enhanced by what happened at the camp. Even from the other lanes, they could see how he worked—walking the deck, talking to his swimmers, timing their laps, not just standing around watching, or talking with other coaches.

The swimming competition of the 1984 Olympic Games was held in the brand-new McDonald's Swim Stadium on the campus of the University of Southern California, in Los Angeles. The swimming facility included a fifty-meter competition pool and a separate diving well, flanked by two huge grandstands. It was the end of July and very hot. There would be over twelve thousand spectators at the competition, the most ever at an Olympic swimming event.

The Olympic Games

The pool was outdoors, and the stadium was ringed with colorful banners and flags: pink, vermilion, magenta, and lavender, all made brighter by the constant sun.

Rowdy Gaines came into the Olympics with a chance of winning three gold medals. One was almost assured: the four-by-hundred freestyle relay, on which Gaines would definitely swim and that the U.S. team was favored to win. The other two medals would be tougher, in part because one depended on the other. If Gaines wanted to swim the anchor leg on the very strong U.S. medley relay—made up of one swimmer doing each of the four strokes—he would have to win the hundred freestyle, or at least defeat Mike Heath of Florida, the other American in the race. Heath had beaten Gaines in the hundred at Trials.

In the morning preliminaries he qualified third, behind Mike Heath and Australia's Mark Stockwell. Gaines warmed down, got dressed, then went back to his room and spent the afternoon trying to relax. He talked for a while with Tracy Caulkins, who could always help him unwind, and watched Woody Woodpecker cartoons and *The Newlywed Game* on television. But, as at the Trials, he was planning to lose the race.

And that, most coaches would say, is a critical mistake. You should aim to win, plan to win, *expect* to win—as Mark Schubert once said, *That is what really separates the very best from everyone else.* Here was Rowdy Gaines, world record holder in the hundred-meter freestyle, the favorite to win three gold medals at the twenty-third Olympic Games, practicing in his mind an athlete's concession speech carefully designed to show the world that he was as gracious in defeat as he had been, for all these years, in victory.

But despite the mental rehearsal of a loser's remarks, Gaines had not been the dominant male sprinter in the world for the past five years by giving up the big races. Despite his repeated hesitations about swimming, his recurring thoughts of retirement, and despite his plans to deal in a mature way with the anticipated defeat at the hands of both Mike Heath and Mark Stockwell, insiders knew that once in the water, Gaines probably would commit himself fully. Sometimes he did lose, but he rarely gave up.

Through the politics of FINA (Féderation Internationale de Natation Amateure), the international body for swimming (which was running the swimming events at the Olympics), Francisco Sylvestri of Panama had been chosen to be the starter for the men's swimming events. He had been the starter at the 1982 World Championships in Cali, Colombia, and at the Caracas 1983 Pan American Games, and both times there had been complaints about him. It seemed he had the habit of telling the swimmers "Take your marks" and then firing the gun very quickly, perhaps before the swimmers had had time to get into their set position. Often it appeared that people were jumping on their starts, as Sylvestri would simply fire the gun and walk away. Protests were made every time, but to no avail. Gaines had been around; he knew who Sylvestri was, and his coach Richard Quick knew; and before the final they talked about it. There would be a "two jump" false-start rule, so nothing would be lost by going off fast once and seizing an advantage.

The last few minutes before the race were the worst. Rowdy tried just lying on his back in the Ready Room set up under a tent behind the pool, looking up at the ceiling. He stood up, and he paced in the front of the electric fans that were in the tent to help the swimmers stay cool in the late afternoon heat. He wished that it were all over, and he tried to calm himself by singing over and over a Phil Collins song, "I Don't Care Anymore." He found the thought relaxing. When the swimmers were marched out onto the deck, Gaines wore a white U.S.A. T-shirt and blue gym shorts over his suit. He was awed by the size of the crowd and then very proud to be here in front of this huge stadium full of people, there to see him swim. When the announcer introduced him, he stepped up to the block and waved, to the cheers of the crowd.

On the blocks, Gaines adjusted his goggles and stood quietly. When Sylvestri, the starter, said "Take your marks," Gaines immediately went down into starting position, bent over with his hands touching the front edge of the starting block. Sylvestri fired the gun. Gaines, anticipating the shot, seemed to start almost before the gun went off; when the videotapes were replayed, they showed clearly that Gaines was holding steady when the gun fired. Mark Stockwell, one lane over, had not yet completely assumed the starting position, was not yet completely down. Combining his readiness with his already remarkable reflexes, Gaines had a clear advantage over everyone else in the field, especially Mike Heath, who even under the best of conditions had a noticeably slow start for a sprinter. Gaines immediately took a healthy lead.

He held it through the turn of the two-lap race. At that point, Gaines was fourteen one-hundredths of a second ahead of Stockwell, a small but significant distance. Gaines knew, he could feel, that he was ahead, but he resisted the temptation to look, knowing that one look, by disturbing his body position and distracting his mind, could cost him the race. Halfway back, as the pain began to build, he thought, *This is my last race, my last twenty-five. Don't stop now.* He wanted to look over to see Heath or Stockwell, and he thought—imagined—the Australian Stockwell to be pulling up on him. He wasn't, but Gaines put his head down and sprinted to the finish. When he stopped, he pulled off his goggles and rested briefly, holding on to the wall in front of him, not daring to turn around and look. All of the other swimmers saw the final results before Gaines. When he eased himself around and looked at the scoreboard, he saw, with apparent surprise, the number

"1" flashed next to his name; he jumped high from the water, threw his fist into the air, laughed and cried and smiled an unbelievable smile. The crowd up in the stands went wild.

In a waiting room behind the swimming pool, Dara Torres sat and watched Gaines' victory on television. She was there with Carrie Steinseifer, preparing for their own swims in the women's four-by-hundred relay, the last event on Tuesday evening. Torres liked Rowdy Gaines, perhaps in a more special way than some other members of the Olympic team, looked up to him as a kind of hero who was also a friend. A year and a half before, when she was just breaking into the top ranks, he had helped her along. His hundred-meter race, just finished, inspired her.

Her morning swim in the preliminaries had not been good. It had been very hot under the tents out behind the pool where the swimmers waited, and while watching the events on television, she became flushed, felt very hot, and got scared. She went into the medical tent, shaking. The attendants there sat her down, gave her drinks, put ice packs on her. By the time of her race she felt okay, but walking out on the deck with the relay team she saw, for the first time, how huge the crowd was, how they roared; she had never swum before such a crowd, had never experienced anything like that. She swam poorly, nervous as she had never been, afraid of doing something wrong.

It was strange, she thought. After the race, despite the nerves and the crowd, she felt fine—very relaxed, very calm, and ready to swim again that evening. It was as if the first swim was needed just to get past the fear of swimming in the Olympic Games to the point of making it, as swimmers sometimes tell each other, "just another swim meet."

Torres and her relay teammates didn't expect the relay itself to be a close race. The American team was favored to win, and the swimmers on it, to get themselves motivated, had set for themselves the goal not just of winning the gold medal but also of breaking the world record. When they walked out onto the deck that evening, as the trumpets played the fanfare especially written for these Games, Torres wore her Walkman, and she was ready to swim. The morning swim had taken off the edge of fear, and she was looking forward to the race. Sometimes in workouts Mark Schubert would tell the Mission Viejo swimmers (and Torres remembered this well) about Brian Goodell, a gold medalist in 1976. Goodell would imagine during practice that he was swimming in the Olympic Games, a little trick to get himself motivated. Torres had done that, too, and sometimes during practice would look up at the stands alongside the pool at Mission, and would imagine the huge crowds there, cheering for the American team, and for her, Dara Torres.

As it happened, they had more of a race than they had expected. After the lead-off swimmers, the team from Holland was in first place; after the second leg, the Americans had an edge; and then Torres dove in the water and swam her leg, the third, against unknown Desi Reijers of Holland.

Torres' time for her swim was 55.92, her fastest hundred ever. Reijers' was 55.62, enough to close to within a tenth of a second, almost dead even with the last leg to go. The Dutch swimmer Connie Van Bentum closed the slight lead on American Nancy Hogshead by the turn, but on the second lap Hogshead, cowinner (in a dead heat) with Steinseifer in the individual hundred freestyle, pulled away to win by almost a second. The American record fell; the world record, held by the East Germans, did not. Without a world record, without even one of the four fastest legs swum, Dara Torres had won an Olympic gold medal.

Mary T. Meagher, the butterflyer, would not swim until Thursday morning, and the waiting was nerve-racking. She was anxious this time, since the expectations for her were so great (a gold medal at least, and preferably a world record). She felt alone, despite the support of her family. Recently she had broken up with her boyfriend, and almost no one else on the American team could sympathize with a swimmer seemingly so dominant. She knew that they didn't need to hear about how tough it was to be heavily favored.

So she spent the first three days of the Olympic competition hearing about how everyone else was doing. She couldn't turn on the television without seeing the Olympics, and by Wednesday evening she had seen friends win and lose and had heard the national anthem more times than she could count. That night she went out for a quiet dinner with her family, came back to the Olympic Village, went to her room, and shaved down—shaving all the hair off of her arms, legs, and back. The purpose of this is not, as some have said, to decrease the "drag" resistance, which is minimal, but rather to increase the skin's sensitivity to water and so improve one's ability to feel where the hands and legs are. It also gives a psychological advantage: It makes you feel faster, feel like you are sliding through the water.

Thursday she faced her biggest challenge: the hundred-meter butterfly. This was the event she lost at Trials to Jenna Johnson, the tall newcomer from California. By Thursday Johnson had already won a gold medal, swimming the lead-off leg on the same four-by-hundred relay that Dara Torres was on. In the relay Johnson had shown again that she was a tremendous sprinter who liked to go out fast in the first fifty meters and try to hang on. Meagher knew that, and knew that she would have to be patient in the race, keeping her stroke together and hoping to catch Johnson on the second fifty. Just to help herself stay calm, Meagher decided not to wear goggles during the race so she wouldn't see Johnson way out ahead.

According to Mark Schubert, Meagher probably had

rested too much for the Trials, lost a little of her feel for the water perhaps, and her stroke had suffered. In the butterfly, as in all the other swimming strokes, "catching" the water is crucial. The pull should start slowly, with a kind of sculling-out movement, before the arm pulls back and moves the body forward. This creates a pause at the start of each arm stroke after the hand enters the water, very noticeable when one first sees world-class swimmers. At the Trials, Meagher had been rushing her pull a bit, not sculling out first, as she should have. The flaw was obvious on the underwater films taken at the Olympic training camp.

But now the problem was corrected. She was sculling out and her head was staying low, so her hips would stay on top of the water. She had tapered for a shorter period than for Trials. Once again Meagher's entire family was in the stands, wearing their "Mary T-shirts" and making noise and waving for the TV cameras.

As expected, Johnson went out very fast, faster than Meagher's world-record split at the fifty. But—and they both knew it would happen this way—as they came back on the second lap, Meagher began to close the gap. In the final ten meters of the race Jenna Johnson began to feel herself giving out, began to "die," and, putting her head down for a stroke, looked back under her and could see Mary T. Meagher coming up fast. Meagher herself, with only a bleary vision (without her goggles) in the last few strokes, just put her own head down and with a quiet prayer of "Oh, please," charged hard and passed Johnson to the wall. Meagher turned, looked up at the enormous electronic scoreboard at the far end of the pool, and saw the time and the "1" next to her name. She won by almost a full second. She sank back and thought, *Thank goodness.* For five years, reporters had asked her—the only thing they had asked her, it seemed—*Will you go to the Los Angeles Olympics? Do you think you can win a gold medal?* She felt, less than happiness, a kind of relief that it was over, that she had finally won an Olympic gold medal five years after first breaking the world record. Finally, she thought, I can live the rest of my life.

The two-hundred butterfly was a walkaway for her as she won by five seconds over a field noticeably weakened by the absence of the East Germans, whom she probably would have beaten anyway. It was still a bittersweet victory, because she didn't quite catch the world record. But it seemed to Mark Schubert that she enjoyed the Games anyway, and that was itself an achievement. From the very beginning, swimming coaches drill into young swimmers' heads this idea that the personal best time is what matters, and sometimes it can take all the fun out of a great career. It seemed to Schubert that at the Olympics Meagher didn't suffer quite so much from that, and that was good.

In the medley relay, where she swam the butterfly leg, the Dutch team had been disqualified for false-starting during the preliminaries, so the race was not close. Meagher swam the fastest hundred meters of butterfly ever swum on a relay (still, the time was slower than her own individual event record from 1981) to finish off the competition.

Afterward she felt that perhaps these had been the last all-out races she might ever swim. Certainly she didn't plan then to repeat the kind of training regimen she had undergone at Mission Viejo over the past ten months. She had three years left as a student at Berkeley, and she would swim on the team there, but more for fun than for glory. She looked forward to that. She was perhaps a little disappointed with her Olympic times, at missing her old world records; but as Schubert said, those times may have been one-time achievements, moments of perfection that one should not expect to be repeated.

By Saturday afternoon, when the fifteen-hundred finals would be swum, other swimmers from Mission Viejo had been disappointed in some small way. Tiffany Cohen had won both the four-hundred and eight-hundred freestyle events, and by substantial margins (three seconds in the four-hundred, five seconds in the eight-hundred), but in both she had just missed, by tenths of a second, the world records set back in 1978 by Australian Tracey Wickham. Ricardo Prado, the Brazilian who had trained at Mission, who had carried his country's flag in the Pan American Games, finished second in the four-hundred individual medley. He had gone out ahead, taken a two-second lead at the halfway mark; but in the breaststroke leg, the third quarter of the race, Canadian Alex Baumann blasted away from the field, leaving Prado and the others behind, to win by more than a full second and set a new world record. Prado, a national hero in his country, brought home a silver, and a fourth place in the two-hundred individual medley.

Despite the fact that his only event came on the last day of the swimming competition, Mike O'Brien enjoyed his week at the Olympics. His ankle seemed to have healed; indeed, his confidence throughout the training-camp period between the Trials and the Games was continually high, as if the injury, like the car wreck on the last day of the Trials, was merely an incident he wouldn't allow to interfere with his plans. There may be physical limitations, he seemed to feel, but this is the Olympic Games; you can't let little things bother you. Instead of fretting over the ankle, or obsessively monitoring his physical condition the way some people would, he spent the better part of the week enjoying the other races, watching some of them on the television in the Olympic Village room he shared with Geoff Gaberino and John Moffet.

O'Brien had never been a big winner. In 1983 he won the five-hundred free at indoor Nationals, but certainly he had never been as strong as DiCarlo or Jeff Kostoff. O'Brien finished well back in the pack at Nationals in 1984, placed fairly well at the U.S.S. International meet before that, and took second in one event at the Olympic Trials. But it never seemed to bother him. He tended, when he talked after a bad swim, to see it rather objectively ("That was a bad swim") but with no emotional upset or anger at himself, just the attitude of *Well, I have to do such-and-such to get better.*

On Thursday morning, in the qualifying heats of the fifteen-hundred free, O'Brien and DiCarlo finished first and fourth, a little less than two seconds apart, with times that would be very slow if either had been trying. But the competition was thin, and both were saving themselves for the finals on Saturday afternoon. Neither wanted to show his cards early.

But for DiCarlo, it was too late to hide. On Thursday he had won the four-hundred free, the event in which he had done so well at Trials. O'Brien, watching DiCarlo, thought then that perhaps his stroke wasn't quite as sharp as it had been in Indianapolis at Trials; his conditioning seemed a little off. Mark Schubert and Mike O'Brien both thought, after watching that race and talking a little, *He could be vulnerable.* Then, too, DiCarlo had already won his Olympic gold medal, and might not be as hungry for the win as O'Brien.

The plan was fairly simple: O'Brien would try, as usual, to stay close to the fast-breaking DiCarlo for the first two hundred meters; stay even for the next five hundred; and then, halfway through the race, "put him away," in Schubert's words.

The crowd of twelve thousand in the Olympic swim stadium at USC could hardly have cared less. The fifteen-hundred is a long, unexciting event for the uninformed, and with two Americans almost certain to win the medals regardless, the few cheers there were never really stirred much enthusiasm. But it didn't matter to O'Brien. In the first hundred meters, trying to go out hard, he clocked a time 1.3 seconds faster than in his first hundred at the Trials; together with DiCarlo, he had a full second lead on third-place Stephan Pfeiffer of West Germany.

By two hundred, DiCarlo and O'Brien had clearly established that it would be a two-man race.

By four hundred they led the rest of the field by three seconds, with DiCarlo a tiny bit ahead. But it was late afternoon in Los Angeles, the sun was hot, the water was a bit warm, and DiCarlo didn't feel good. "My stroke hasn't felt right at this meet," he would say later. O'Brien's analysis of the four-hundred free had been correct: DiCarlo was not in top form, he wasn't up to his best shape. Between the six-hundred- and the thousand-meter marks, O'Brien moved ahead, very steadily, until he was two seconds ahead, and then, by twelve hundred meters, three seconds ahead—a lead of about sixteen feet, apparently insurmountable over the short distance remaining to swim. By then the struggling DiCarlo was contending with a late charge by Pfeiffer, who gained with each lap.

For the last three hundred meters, O'Brien tried only to stay calm, not to panic, not to fall apart the way he had a year before at the Pan American Games. There he had led the fifteen-hundred with only three hundred to go, had it wrapped up he thought, and he had simply fallen apart and finished fourth. *Relax, keep it going*, he thought. With a hundred meters to go, the crowd came alive, and O'Brien went for the finish. He won the race, finally, by five seconds. DiCarlo finished second, Pfeiffer third.

Later, on the victory stand, with the gold medal hanging around his neck, O'Brien would reach his long arms high into the air, stretched above him, his index fingers extended into "1" signs; his face beamed with boyish enthusiasm. He was eighteen years old, soon to become a freshman at the University of Southern California, where his swimming team would train right here in this pool. This was his pool, and this was his day. He loved the crowds, the flags, the band, the national anthem. It was, he would recall, "the greatest thing in my life."

The Olympic Games turned the swimming world inside out. From being directed inward toward itself, a small community of friends and rivals looking to each other for recognition, swimming became one part of a tremendous entertainment production overseen by a massive organization (including some seventy thousand volunteer workers), the Los Angeles Olympic Organizing Committee.

As the sport turns outward, the audience becomes the most important actor. In professional sports in America, whenever there is a baseball strike, for instance, appeals are made to how *this is really for the fans,* or *the fans are really what this is all about,* etc. Complaints are made on the other side, that *this really hurts the fans.* No such arguments arise in swimming. The sport is for the swimmers, the "kids." Whether this is practiced consistently or not, it is seen as the legitimate purpose of the sport. It is seen as proper that the athletes' good should be the primary consideration. This certainly is not the case in professional sports. At the Olympics, the ticket prices were thirty-five dollars for the prime seats in the swimming stadium in the morning preliminary events and up to ninety dollars and above for the premium seats in the finals. The stands were filled either with fanatic swimming fans (or, more likely, parents and coaches of the athletes) or with people who simply wanted to see "the Olympics," whatever the sport, and who were willing to spend the money. There were over 12,100 people in the swim stadium on the final day of swimming (Saturday night) at Los Angeles, the largest group ever at an Olympics and certainly the largest spectator body—and the noisiest—that the athletes had ever competed in front of.

The swimming races were run as spectator-oriented

events, in the European style. No swimmers were allowed
on the deck (the area around the pool itself) until immediately before their events. They were escorted out to the
pool, each with their own "valet," an Olympic volunteer
who would watch the athlete's warm-up suit and equipment bag during the event. After introductions to the spectators, the event would be swum, and the athletes paraded
back out the gate into the waiting area under some tents.
Except for officials—whose physical positions around the
pool were carefully specified—there were no other people
on the deck, save the television people. Even the press
photographers were kept under the front of the stands, in a
narrow canvas bunker, from which they could snap away
while not getting too close to the athletes. Coaches were
barred from the deck at any time during the competition
itself. The national teams were seated off the end of the
competition pool—on the far end, in fact, of the diving
pool—so they weren't able to see the finish of any races
at all but had to look up at the scoreboard to see who
had won.

The spectators seemed, by comparison with those at
other major swim meets, relatively ignorant of the sport—
primarily curiosity-seekers eager to see what these people
looked like. At a high-school or college meet, spectators
were largely parents, and fellow students at the school.
U.S.S. crowds tended to be quiet but informed; the school
crowds, noisy. Here at the Olympics people had to ask who
Tracy Caulkins was, what the individual medley is, and
the like. At one morning's preliminaries, on the front row
of the stands, a middle-aged man came in a half hour after
the events began, sat down, and opened a *Los Angeles
Times*, which he read for the rest of the morning. Another
couple nearby, perhaps in their twenties, were pointedly
bored throughout, talking to each other and looking around
at the crowd. There were differences, too, between the
morning spectators at the preliminaries and the afternoon

finals audiences (who paid more and were more genteel). The preliminaries were less important and less expensive; the crowds there were relatively noisy and waved flags; the mood was raucous, sometimes even obnoxious. One middle-aged fellow in the stands wore a cap on the bill of which was printed, with charming simplicity, "Fuck Russia."

In general, the crowds at the swim stadium were vigorously pro-American, waving huge flags and chanting "U!S!A! U!S!A!" at every opportunity. Their identification with the athletes was not on the basis of ability—if that were true, then Michael Gross of West Germany, probably the outstanding male swimmer of the meet, would have received the greatest applause—but on the basis of national affiliation. Relays by their nature were team-oriented and thus more obviously represented a country than any particular person could, so they received by far the greatest enthusiasm from the crowds. After the men's eight-hundred freestyle relay, in which the Americans narrowly defeated the Gross-anchored West Germans, Jeff Float, an American swimmer who has been 80 percent deaf since childhood, won much favor with the press with his comment "The noise was deafening."

The cheering was, for the most part, simply pro-United States. Were the people in the stands to have identified with sports, the great cheers would be for Jon Sieben's two-hundred fly, or Tracy Caulkins' four-hundred IM, or Gross's two-hundred free. But they weren't. Despite what the athletes themselves said about how great it was to receive recognition, there was little real "recognition" in the sense of the spectators recognizing who the athletes were and what they had really accomplished. Instead, up in the grandstands on those hot afternoons, there was a diffuse sort of excitement that "one of us" has done well. The athletes merely provided the impetus and the opportunity for that excitement.

The Olympic Games

11

A New Mission

ROWDY GAINES RETIRED FROM SWIMMING IMMEDIATELY
after the 1984 Olympic Games. He hired an agent, Parkes
Brittain of the Advantage International Agency in Washington, D.C., and began a four-year whirlwind of touring.
Sometimes he was on the road for seven weeks at a time: to
Reno for a weekend swim meet, then a week-long conference in Colorado for *Sports Illustrated* advertisers, then
jumping on a jet down to Florida for visits at a chain of
Hardee's restaurants with Olympic gymnast Peter Vidmar
to promote the Special Olympics. Then Gaines was off to
give a series of inspirational speeches sponsored by Merrill
Lynch Realty, an Olympic team sponsor; he would put in
an appearance at the U.S. Open Tennis Championships in
Flushing Meadow, New York, give more speeches (these
sponsored by Blue Cross/Blue Shield, in Pittsburgh), and
then fly back to New York, perhaps for an Oleg Cassini ad
shooting or an appearance on the sports network, ESPN. It

was financially rewarding (one could make thousands of dollars a day on such a schedule) and fun. He also took a job as head coach of an age-group swim team in Las Vegas but soon found that the celebrity business kept him on the road far too much to do an adequate job of coaching. At one point he became sick from the exhausting schedule. But he did enjoy it all, and he knew that after the 1988 Olympic Games in Seoul, South Korea, his professional career as a gold medalist would slow down considerably, as he would be replaced by a younger star.

In the fall of 1984, returning to college after the year of training for and competing in the Olympics, Mary T. Meagher went to the coach of the women's swim team at Cal-Berkeley, Karen Moe Thornton (herself a gold medalist from 1972, also in the butterfly), and said that she wanted to quit swimming. She was tired of the hard training and the time away from her other activities. She wanted to join clubs, and play other sports for fun, and go to some fraternity parties, even if she did feel a little awkward at them. She wanted to be a college student, not a swimmer, for a while.

Thornton understood, but she needed her star to stay. She suggested that Meagher remain a member of the team, help them out at meets, and just work out two days a week, enough to keep her feel of the water. Meagher knew that this was an unusual proposition coming from a college coach, the sort of person who usually demands complete dedication. She appreciated the offer and took it. She was able to help, and continued, even with less training, to win college championships. She continued swimming with reduced workouts until the spring of 1987, when she quit training altogether for a while. Finally her NCAA eligibility expired; she had done her part for Cal, and now she could accept payment for promotions and actually make some money from her swimming success. She began traveling the country, once a week or so on average (though nothing like the grueling full-time work Rowdy Gaines was pursuing), promoting Speedo swimsuits and holding clinics. She also moved back to Louisville, Kentucky, to live with her family. She joined a Nautilus club, took up playing tennis and golf, and generally enjoyed herself.

She liked doing the promotional stints. It gave her a chance to meet parents and children who looked up to her, to catch a glimpse of their world and how they saw swimming. She would show them one of her gold medals with the event name engraved on the edge; they would be surprised at how heavy it was and ask her for an autograph or some bit of advice. Some wanted her to sign their bathing caps, and many parents wanted to know what college scholarships for swimming were available and how good their child had to be to win one. As the conversations grew more serious, Meagher had a chance to teach people a little bit about her sport.

But she learned something, too, and sometimes it surprised her. "They don't understand how ordinary it is to be a good swimmer . . ." she would say. "They think it takes a special team, or a special personality . . . [but] you can start right in your own backyard or in a summer league. It doesn't take a magic potion." She tried to tell disbelieving parents how Rowdy Gaines didn't start serious competitive swimming until he was in high school, or how she herself started out in a country-club league. She tried to tell them not to push their kids, not to plan their child's career, that it didn't work that way. She had become excellent, she believed, by doing fairly ordinary things consistently and with care. She was better than most swimmers, she thought, because she worked hard and enjoyed it; because she had always taken care of herself, never gotten into drugs or alcohol (there was no self-sacrifice involved in this; she had never wanted to use drugs), never stayed out late, exhausting herself running around; because her family supported her and helped her have fun in the sport; and because of a whole series of mundane habits she had developed over the years: "I never do an illegal turn," she said, not even in workouts. She would, in her early years, push herself harder as she became more tired, as the workout went on. She would find herself looking at the other kids in workouts, watching to see as they began to fade, and then she would start pushing herself more, knowing that this was the advantage. It was those things that made her great: the love of hard work, the consistency, the natural self-discipline, the concentration on always doing things a little better than everyone else.

In retrospect, her fabulous success seemed an almost unexpected outcome of her diligence. She certainly hadn't planned at the beginning to become a great athlete. She hadn't meant to get so serious about swimming; she hadn't known, early on, just what it would entail. "I never knew that I would be practicing five or six hours a day, and if I would have known, I would have never . . ."

Then she would pause. "I look back now and think, 'How did I ever do that? That's ridiculous; no one should ever do that.'"

But at the time, as she was just becoming a national-level swimmer—in fact, throughout her career—"I never looked beyond the next year, and I never looked beyond the next level. I never thought about the Olympics when I was ten. At that time I was thinking about the State Championships. When I made cuts for Regionals, I started thinking about Regionals; when I made cuts for National Junior Olympics, I started thinking NJO's. I never even knew anything like Nationals existed . . . I can't even think about the Olympics right now [June 1987]." At every stage she had looked only a short distance ahead, setting goals that would not overwhelm her.

After 1984, her concentration on swimming diminished. Working out with the team at Cal or training during the summers with the Lakeside Aquatics team in Louisville, she found that as the pain would build, she would back off a little, just ease up a bit, both mentally and physically. The drive wasn't there anymore, no more reason to chase down the leaders, to win every set. It was mainly just being older: She had known the great thrills already, and they weren't as exciting as before. She knew she could do it if she wanted. She had set world records, won Olympic gold medals—three of them—and countless times, it seemed, she had won National Championship titles. Still, she continued swimming, in part because she was so successful at it and the rewards kept coming, in part because she enjoyed the exercise, which made her feel strong and healthy, and in part because she felt like she was making her own special contribution, doing something worthwhile with her life. She knew she would marry, settle down, and have children. Maybe her kids would swim, and maybe they wouldn't. It wouldn't matter to her at all, as long as they had fun.

She thought sometimes about the 1988 Olympics. There were two reasons for her to go: first, to beat the East Germans at their best; and second, to become the first woman to make the American team in the same event for three successive Olympics. This thought intrigued her, but she was willing to wait and see, never thinking seriously more than a few months ahead. Sometimes a young man she liked would kid her about the 1992 Olympics. She would laugh, and brush off the comment as a friendly joke; then she would think about it for a moment or two and smile.

In the fall of 1984, Mike O'Brien began his freshman year at the University of Southern California in Los Angeles. He quickly came to love college. He was a hard worker, a friendly guy who loved having new friends, horsing around in the dorm, talking politics with other students. He and his roommate that year, Chris Hansen, made funny tapes for their telephone answering machine. O'Brien, away from his mother's healthy cooking for the first time, began to lose his preoccupation with nutrition; he ate more hamburgers and potato chips, more junk food and fewer vegetables than had been his habit. He loved collegiate swimming, too, with its intense dual-meet season. The workouts were shorter than Schubert's had been, but more challenging, because he was racing all the time with other men his own age. And he loved the camaraderie of the USC squad, more close-knit probably than a club team, and the aggressive spirit of the team. With his tremendous background of three years of world-class training in the Animal Lane at the Marguerite pool, O'Brien came to dominate the distance events throughout the winter season at USC. By March of that year, O'Brien broke the American records in both the five-hundred- and thousand-yard freestyles. Finally, in the spring of 1985, at the U.S.S. Spring National Championships, he won three events, finished fourth in another, and walked away with the men's High Point Trophy, becoming unofficially the "most valuable swimmer" at the meet.

For a year now he had been undefeated in his major events. *Swimming World* magazine ran a cover story on him, with a handful of photos and a slew of complimentary quotations from friends and admirers in the sport. Everyone said what a great guy he was, extolled his polite manner, his personal kindness; the information director of U.S.S. said, "This is the type of person we need representing United States Swimming."

Eventually, though, the rush and turmoil caught up with him. The constant pressure to perform, deteriorating nutrition, a new, less disciplined lifestyle, the post-Olympic celebrity round of clinics, black-tie dinners, and Republican party galas, magazine articles, interviews, travel; and schoolwork on top of it all began to take their toll. Only one week after the Nationals, O'Brien finally lost a fifteen-hundred-meter freestyle race, in the Monaco International Meet. In fact, he failed even to make the finals. Crashing down from a lofty height, he became seriously ill for four weeks, primarily from exhaustion. The illness gradually eased into a long low spell during which his motivation for swimming all but disappeared. In a way, as he looked back on it later, the slump should not have been a surprise. For years he had looked forward to the Nationals, the Olympic Trials, the Olympic Games. Now, for the first time in years, Mike O'Brien had no dreams to reach for, no new goals to excite him. During that summer of 1985 he headed back to Mission Viejo, hoping there to regain some of his former enthusiasm. He started working again in the Animal Lane in mid-May, but he was no longer accustomed to swimming twenty thousand meters a day. He soon developed a shoulder problem. O'Brien thought the soreness was partly psychological, just one more expression of his failing interest; and competitively he performed poorly. The next winter season was a continuing disappointment as he slipped lower and lower in the national rankings. In the summer of 1986 he managed to win a place on the U.S. World Championship team, but after arriving in Madrid he contracted a stomach flu and dropped out of his only event, the men's eight-hundred-meter freestyle relay.

None of this made much sense to him, but he continued hoping for some sort of answer. It came at the end of the year. On Christmas Eve of 1986 he was eating dinner with his girlfriend's family when her father, a dentist, noticed that Mike's jaw was clicking as he ate. The man asked about it, whether it was chronic. It was. He referred O'Brien to a friend who was a chiropractor. After a thorough examination, the chiropractor found O'Brien to be suffering from TMJ ("temporomandibular joint") syndrome, a malfunction of the jaw sometimes caused by grinding of the teeth—itself a sign of stress. The jaw malfunction made eating more difficult, unpleasant sometimes.

The diagnosis was a clear signal. It told him, for the first time, what had happened during the two years since the Games. He realized the pressure he had been under, how he had not taken care of himself, how he had not been eating well. He realized now the demands that college, for all the fun, had made on him, and perhaps how he had let himself be swept away. As a result, O'Brien cut back on the heavy training and began rebuilding his old good habits, the ones that had helped him during the year before the Olympics. He tried some new events in swim meets—the sprints, even—that required less training; he gained weight (fifteen pounds over what he had weighed in 1984), picked up speed, relaxed a bit, and began enjoying himself again. He became more active in the politics of U.S. Swimming, where he was an athlete representative, an elected member of the Board of Directors. In the summer of 1987, training with Mark Schubert, O'Brien made the Pan American Games team (as he had done four years earlier), and in the two-hundred-meter backstroke he swam a time that would have made the finals in the 1984 Olympic Games. It was an event he had never swum before in international competition. At the Pan American Games held at Indianapolis in August 1987, Michael O'Brien won the gold medal in the two-hundred-meter backstroke.

It seemed to him then that he could go to the Seoul Olympics in 1988. He had a new event, a fresh approach, and a returning sense of what fun swimming could be. He set new goals, at least for now: to make the U.S. Olympic team in four events: the two-hundred-meter backstroke; the two-hundred free; the four-hundred free; and his old favorite, his gold-medal event from 1984, the fifteen-hundred-meter freestyle. *Four events*, he thought: That was a worthy goal. And the thought of it, at this trying time in his life, gave Mike O'Brien renewed courage.

*   *   *

When Dara Torres returned to her prep school in Los Angeles in the fall of 1984, she discovered that the Olympic Games were not just another swim meet. Kids in the hallways would whisper and look when she walked by; people wanted to ask her about her summer; the more curious asked to see her gold medal. There were television appearances, too, and banquets, and she became something of a celebrity, at least locally. One day the headmaster of her school asked if she would bring her gold medal for him to see, in its case. She did; he asked if he could keep it for the day. And that morning at the opening assembly, with the seniors (including Torres) sitting on the stage as tradition required, facing the other students, the headmaster stood up and made a little speech about how one student at the school did something different over the summer—she won an Olympic gold medal. He had Dara stand up in front of everyone, and he hung the medal around her neck. All the students and teachers applauded. Torres was embarrassed, not quite used to such attention. From then on, students came up to her frequently and asked her about the Games and wanted to see her medal. She saw herself as the same person, but how others saw her had been magically transformed.

She didn't swim that fall. Instead she went out for the other sports she loved, volleyball and basketball. She enjoyed sleeping late, not having to drag herself out of bed early every day for morning workouts. She no longer smelled like chlorine all day. She enjoyed going out with friends on weekends and generally being a normal person. In the spring of her senior year, she looked over the best swimming schools and, realizing she was not a strong student academically, ruled out Stanford and then the University of Texas. For several months she flipflopped between the University of Southern California and the University of Florida. USC was close to home; she had trained with Don Lamont,

A New Mission

the coach there, and liked him. On the other hand, her father wanted her to visit Florida; Florida had Randy Reese, and he was tough and good. His team did innovative workouts, they seemed very scientific, and maybe she needed someone very strong to guide her. Reese took her out to lunch during the spring Nationals, told her about Florida swimming and the journalism program there (she was interested in that), and he impressed her. On the last day of the meet, after much worrying, she decided to go to Florida.

For Dara Torres, Florida would not be like Mission Viejo. At Mission she had been a star, the great sprinter on a team of distance swimmers. But at Florida she was one of many great sprinters, and Reese was not a man to defer to her anyway. He gave her very tough workouts, pushed her to race against others in practice, trained her for longer events than just the fifty and the hundred. He made her get down on all fours, with wheels under her knees, and walk using her hands up and down the ramps at the Florida football stadium; he made her swim with a rope around her waist, rigged to a pulley full of weights that held her back, across the pool in the O'Connell Athletic Center. He monitored her weight, talked to her about her diet, pushed her to swim races she didn't like swimming. Initially her swimming performance was no better; it took her a while to adjust to the new program. But by her second year at Florida, Reese's approach was paying off: Torres was stronger and her endurance was better. She could swim the hundred without fading, and even her two-hundred was becoming very respectable.

By 1987 she would be more serious about swimming than ever before in her life. At fifteen, success had come so easily: she'd step up on the starting blocks, dive in, and break a world record. Now, at twenty, the sport was much harder. She had to train more; watch her weight and her diet; take care of her knees (which had suffered multiple injuries and surgical operations); and deal with the distractions of college life, which she relished. She was certainly more mature in her training. She no longer horsed around, as she sometimes had at Mission, sitting on the bottom of the pool in the middle of sets in practice, or sneaking as many as a dozen Twinkies into her room for snacks. Now she would "lead the lane," going ahead of the other swimmers during practice, racing with the best of the men. And she found, to her surprise, that she enjoyed swimming more. She had found some new appreciation for the sport, and she looked forward to the Seoul Games. Perhaps she was hungrier than some others, with something more to prove. Yes, she had won a gold medal, but the East Germans hadn't been there, and it wasn't the individual hundred free but a relay. Some people had said that Dara Torres was a drop-dead sprinter who couldn't go the full distance. But Torres knew she could go faster, a lot faster, and maybe with Reese's training and her new enthusiasm for the sport she could break another world record.

In the summer of 1987 Dara Torres won the hundred-meter freestyle at the Long Course Nationals; then she went to the Pan Pacific Games in Australia, swam the hundred-meter free there in 55.8 seconds, her lifetime best, and won the gold medal. For Dara Torres, no longer a child, competitive swimming was better than ever.

In August 1985, Mark Schubert left Mission Viejo, California, to take a new coaching position, in Boca Raton, Florida. There, about ten miles inland from the Atlantic Ocean, a developer named Jim Brady was building a 565-acre planned community with hundreds of town houses and single-family dwellings, thirteen major lakes, nine residential "villages," parks, recreational facilities, day-care centers, and its own theme shopping center. Finally—and this was the attraction for Mark Schubert—at the center of this whole production would be a world-class aquatic training center. The community would be called Mission

Bay and was explicitly modeled after Mission Viejo. When Brady began planning Mission Bay he called in Schubert as a consultant, saying he wanted his new project to feature the best outdoor swim training facility in the country and he wanted Schubert to design it. Schubert did, building the complex to his own dream specifications: two fifty-meter pools, a twenty-five-yard teaching pool, a huge diving well with eight springboards and numerous platforms, spectator seating for four thousand people (including an enclosed press and VIP box), broadcast facilities, meeting rooms, locker rooms, weight training rooms, and a complete sports physiology and medicine laboratory. Jim Brady was impressed and told Schubert he was also looking for a coach. Did Schubert know anyone? Schubert suggested himself, and was hired.

Since the 1984 Olympics, he had frequently thought of leaving Mission Viejo. His goals there had been achieved: His team had won the National Championships, and Schubert had created the best competitive swimming program in America. He had coached Olympic gold medalists and world record holders. There was little more to accomplish there. He briefly considered going into business, doing something else for a change, but when the Mission Bay opportunity came along, it was too good to pass up. He would have the very best facilities, including some that Mission Viejo had lacked (locker rooms, labs, extra pools). Beyond that, coaching in Florida was itself a challenge. The East Coast was not the great pressure cooker of swimming competition that California was; while there were large numbers of fairly good swimmers, the really world-class competition was limited, and perhaps Schubert saw that, too, as a new challenge, to bring world-class attitudes to the region.

In the summer of 1986, the pools at Mission Bay were not yet built, and it was unclear where the team would train. Still, a number of swimmers, including Olympians

Mike O'Brien and Amy White, came to Boca Raton to work with Schubert. He had to rent pools all over the southern Florida coast, thirteen pools in all, jumping hither and yon from week to week, just trying to keep his team in the water. They lived in the dorms at Florida International University in Miami. At the end of that crazy summer, the Mission Bay Makos went to the National Championships and won the women's team title and the overall team title. For the second time, Mark Schubert had taken a team from the bottom to the top.

The victory was a tremendous vindication for him. For years he had heard the jokes of how Mission Viejo was "the best team that money could buy"; he knew the resentment against his program, knew that many coaches believed his success came from the recruiting of other coaches' swimmers, from his control over the Marguerite pools, from the corporate money that the Mission Viejo Company poured into the team. Now here was the proof otherwise: It was the great program, his method for developing great athletes, that brought success. The money didn't do it, nor the pool, nor even the location of the team. Sure, some great swimmers had come out to Boca Raton to help, but they came neither for the money (there was none at that point) nor for the pools (again, there was no team pool, good or bad). They came because they had faith in Mark Schubert and his assistants. It was the commitment, the coaches, the program that really mattered.

Sometimes Schubert would think back to Akron, Ohio, where he grew up and where he began coaching. He remembered battling "the mentality," as he called it, of the parents and the kids who said "You can't do it in Akron." They had never given him the chance, really, because they were so sure it wasn't possible to be a great swimmer in Akron. But he had managed to convince a few, Terry Stoddard and several of the other boys from the Cuyahoga Falls Black Tiger high-school team. When he moved to California, he had taken them with him. When the swimmers at Mission Viejo saw Stoddard and the others doing the workouts, they began to think, *Well, if these guys can do it, so can I.* The entire team swam better. Then Peggy Tosdal and Valerie Lee joined the team, then Shirley Babashoff and Brian Goodell, and soon Mission Viejo, using one great swimmer to draw another, had leapfrogged its way to the top of American swimming and even of world swimming. At each level Schubert tried to show his swimmers that they could be better, that it was possible to do the tougher workouts, to swim the faster sets, to beat the bigger stars.

"So few kids can accept the fact [that they can be world-class]," he would say. "Everyone bad-raps the big program," he would explain, "but swimming in the same lane with a world record holder or a world champion made it so much easier for them to accept that they could be like that, [to think] 'That's just another kid like me, I keep up with him in practice. . . .'" Schubert constantly worked to make that vision. For all those years he consistently tried to show his swimmers what excellence actually looked like, day to day, so they could believe, *I could do that.*

At Mission Bay in 1986, with three pools side by side, he could put his entire team—hundreds of swimmers—in the water at the same time. While a world record holder was in lane seven, a ten-year-old was in lane one, just learning the butterfly. Every so often that ten-year-old could look over and see what a world record holder looked like and could get to know that person, see her every day in practice. The mixture of reality and dreams was fantastic, exciting; the whole range was right in front of Schubert. He loved, too, just having the small children around the pool; he loved having his own two little daughters, coming into practice and walking by him and giggling or sometimes stopping to give him a hug.

He was more relaxed than before. His shoulders moved more loosely, he laughed more often and more easily.

Sometimes, in earlier years—the late 1970s, especially— coaching had been hard for Mark Schubert. He coached great athletes, to be sure, but sometimes they were hard to manage, and always there was his concern for drawing the line. Now he knew who he was and what he was doing, really felt confident in both himself and his work, in what he could do as a coach. The swimmers knew it, too. *They want it so badly,* he thought, watching the kids in Florida training. Soon the Mission Bay Training Center would have its own sports psychologist, nutritionist, and physiologist; they would bring in scientists to conduct lactate testing and body composition testing. In 1988, he knew, there would be another Olympic Games; and Mark Schubert and a good number of his swimmers planned to be there.

A New Mission

EPILOGUE

The Mundanity of Excellence

THE CHAMPION ATHLETE DOES NOT SIMPLY DO MORE OF THE same drills and sets as other swimmers; he or she also does things *better*. That's what counts. Very small differences, consistently practiced, will produce results. In swimming it could be doing all turns legally, or swimming one extra set of repeats after practice every day, or wearing gloves on your hands to keep them warm at a meet. American historian John Morton Blum reportedly has said that to be successful a writer need produce only three pages a day—every single day. Often the trick is doing little things (like good turns) correctly, all the time, every time. Championship training consists of doing more and more of these little things—and they are, finally, innumerable—each one consistently, so that each one produces a result.

The results of such quality training inevitably add up. Swimming is swimming, we can say—in practice, or in meets, it's all the same. If you swim sloppily for 364 days a year, nothing great is going to happen on the day of that one big meet, no matter how excited you get. Nowadays top-level swimmers tend to treat workouts as meets, where every swim counts; they have to win each repeat, always do great starts and turns. Steve Lundquist, for example, decided early in his career to try to win every swim in every practice, and eventually he did that. Many Mission Viejo swimmers took time every day to psych up for workouts, which they treated as intense competitions. It was not uncommon to see swimmers at Mission Viejo swimming within seconds of their lifetime bests in practices, going all out every day. When they eventually got to a meet, there was nothing new to be overcome, and the conclusion was all but foregone: For all the closeness of the times at Nationals, the same people often do win, year after year.

When Rowdy Gaines studied the starter in the Olympic Games, that was not a new "trick" he invented that day. He always checked the starter, as do many swimmers, because he knows that sometimes it makes a difference. He wasn't "cheating" to win that day. He was simply attending to details that other people didn't, and he had the good luck that the officials didn't recall the start. Mike Heath and Mark Stockwell and the five other swimmers in that race could have anticipated the gun, too, perhaps with good results, but they didn't. Gaines did.

These little things matter not so much because of their physical impact but because psychologically they separate the champion from everyone else. Having done the little things, the champion can say "I have done what no one else has done, and I know it; and they know it, too." The little things, the details, then can be important for their testimonial value, their symbolic value, in setting one apart as someone special or different—someone to be watched and to be paid attention to. "This guy takes this seriously (and we don't); he really does deserve to win." "Why should I hurt myself in this race when Christine wants it that bad?"

The little things, far from being an aggravation for top-level athletes, are the part they most enjoy: the polished points that mark the craftsmen of sport.

One result of this we call "confidence." Some people believe that confidence is "mental" or is "all in your head," as if you could just, one day, decide to have it. Or they believe that you get "confidence" when you buy a cassette tape that tells you to *relax, think positively, visualize your races,* and so on. They believe that confidence is a mental trick, like hypnosis, that can take one to incredible feats. But the confidence of the champion is not some trick learned by listening to an inspiring lecture. Confidence is not the cause of championship; it is the result of setting up difficult tasks and then doing them. As one coach put it, "Mental preparation is something you do in the water every day."

Our usual view of champions tells us the opposite. We think they are special people, larger than life: unusually good-looking, successful, happy all the time, patriotic, and self-confident. Failures don't get much TV coverage. For the sake of drama, reasonably enough, storytellers enhance some parts of the story and downplay others. And we think reasonably: *My God, this guy is nothing like me, I could never do what he does.*

But there is no magic that separates Olympians from everyday people, despite the fact that the title suggests Greek gods. No one is born to make the Olympic finals; potential doesn't win a gold medal. Doing it is the only thing that counts. The truth is simple: Most swimmers choose every day not to do the little things. They choose, in effect, not to win. They say, "I could do this workout if I wanted to," or "I could have rolled with the start," or "I would have won if I had been healthy." In some sense, everyone "could" win in the Olympic Games, but "could" doesn't count. The gold medal is reserved for those who *do.*

The Mundanity of Excellence

The *doing*—this alone makes champions different. The excitement they feel comes from the raw physical and emotional reality they face every morning as they swim six miles, paying attention to all the details. Certainly the Olympic Games represent a rare opportunity to demonstrate publicly one's heroic capabilities. But champions do not wait four years to find their heroic opportunities; they create those opportunities, every day.

A Spectator's Guide to the 1988 Olympic Games

BARRING POLITICAL UPHEAVAL IN SOUTH KOREA OR AN EASTern bloc boycott, the swimming competition in Seoul should be better than that in the 1984 Los Angeles Games. In Los Angeles, the absence of the East German and Soviet teams thinned the competition, allowing the American women in particular to take numerous medals in freestyle and relay events, that they could not have won otherwise. But in Seoul, with the D.D.R.'s powerful team in top shape, and with other countries fielding gold-medal contenders in select events, world records should be set in many events, and making the final eight will be tough.

Swimming competition is improving generally and this will show up in the Olympics. In the 1960s the United States would often sweep Olympic events, taking 1-2-3, both in men's and women's. Now that *cannot* happen. The rules limit each nation to two entrants per event—and it likely *would* not happen even with unlimited entrants.

Other countries are stronger. The West German men, led by "The Albatross," six-foot-six Michael Gross, hold the world record in the four-by-two-hundred freestyle relay, which shows their strength in the middle distances; Australian women threaten world records in longer events; the Dutch women, before being disqualified in the preliminaries (for "jumping"—one swimmer took off before the previous one touched), had a strong chance of winning the medley relay in Los Angeles; the Soviets are always strong in breaststroke. Canadian Victor Davis took one gold and one silver medal in Los Angeles and is still competing. The Olympics are no longer merely an international showcase for American talent.

In addition, swimmers are staying in the sport longer. In the 1960s, many American women would quit swimming at sixteen or seventeen. Now, thanks to Title IX and a wider acceptance of women's sports, they stay, competing in college and in multiple Olympics. More scientifically sophisticated training methods allow athletes to maintain conditioning for years with less training; a good number of male sprinters continue competing well into their late twenties. All of this means tougher, more experienced swimmers in the competition.

Still, there are a handful of American swimmers whose prospects seem good, and who will almost certainly be among the strong finalists at Seoul. Potential heroes include the following.

THE MEN'S EVENTS

The West Germans, Canadians, East Germans, and Soviets are particularly strong, although overall the United States probably has the best team. Relay events should be heartstoppers, with several different nations going for the win in each.

Matt Biondi

If there is to be a "Mark Spitz of 1988," his name is Matt Biondi. In 1984, at eighteen years old, Biondi became one of those anomalies to make the Olympic Team without any national reputation. He had played on the NCAA championship water-polo team at the University of California at Berkeley, but the Olympic Games was his first big international swim meet. When told that Matt Biondi would be the fourth swimmer on the American four-by-hundred free-style relay, Rowdy Gaines reportedly said, "Matt who?"

Since then, Biondi has quickly eclipsed Gaines as the dominant sprint freestyler in the world, smashing Gaines's record in the hundred and ranking almost a full second ahead of anyone else in the world in the event in 1987. He also owns the American record in the two-hundred free. His stroke is technically flawless, even beautiful. An underwater view of his pull reveals no bubbles coming off of his hands—a sign that he places his hands in the water smoothly and is pulling on water, not air. Add to that his tremendous strength: Standing six feet six inches tall and weighing two hundred pounds—heavy for a swimmer— Biondi moves his arms slowly, taking fewer strokes per length of the pool than most of his competitors, sliding along gracefully. Whatever he loses in "low turnover" (how fast he moves his arms), he gains through power and technique.

He does have weaknesses. His start and turns are poor, for one. While the long-course competition of the Olympics favors a swimmer like Biondi, he is very vulnerable in the fifty free (a new Olympic event for 1988) to Tom Jager from UCLA, who holds the world record only hundredths of a second ahead of Biondi.

Biondi is a "second half" swimmer: If he leads at the fifty in a one-hundred-meter race, he will probably win. But at distances over one hundred, his endurance is not that of, say, West Germany's Michael Gross. For Biondi to match Spitz's seven gold medals, he would need near-perfect training and then some luck. The fifty he could win, but the start is crucial, and that is a weak point for him. In the hundred he will be favored, with his power and distance per stroke paying off in the fifty-meter pool. In the two-hundred, Michael Gross is a more likely winner, but if Gross has a bad day and Biondi a good one, it could go the other way. Then, as the top U.S. hundred free swimmer, Biondi will likely anchor both the sprint freestyle and the medley relays, both of which the United States should win.

That would make five gold medals, assuming everything goes right. The last two medals to tie Spitz would demand something extraordinary. In the four-by-two-hundred freestyle relay, which Biondi will likely anchor, the West Germans, with Gross's "fastest-ever relay leg," hold the world record. The East German men, until recently a relatively unknown quantity, are less than a second behind (the event lasts around seven minutes); and the Americans, judging from recent international meets, are close behind that. But in so long a race, and in so important a meet, the United States could finish anywhere from first to third.

Biondi's last chance for a medal will come in the hundred-meter butterfly. At this writing, he is the second fastest in the world. But number one, the unchallenged world-record holder, is fellow American Pablo Morales, and this is his event.

It also should be said that Michael Gross could match Spitz's seven medals, winning most of them against Biondi. Watch for their head-to-head races in the two-hundred free, the hundred fly, and all the relays. Biondi has the speed, Gross the endurance.

Pablo Morales

Pablo Morales, son of Cuban emigrés and a veteran of international swimming, will be twenty-four when the Seoul

Olympics are held. He graduated from Stanford in 1987, where he won more NCAA national championships than any other swimmer in history. He holds the world record in the hundred-meter butterfly—he held it in 1984, but finished second in the Olympic finals behind Michael Gross. He also won the Olympic silver medal in the two-hundred-meter individual medley. He holds the American record in the two-hundred butterfly and the two-hundred individual medley record. With Olympic experience and number-one world ranking, he has to be favored in the hundred fly; in the two-hundred, Gross will probably win, and Morales could battle it out for second with a half-dozen others. In the two-hundred IM, he generally has a huge lead—more than a full second—over world-record pace after the butterfly, and stays close during the backstroke; he then fades through the breaststroke and freestyle, but can often still win. If Morales doesn't have a large (say, two-second) lead after the backstroke, count him out. The other men in the medleys are great breaststroke swimmers.

Note: in the hundred fly, Morales's attack will come against Biondi's weakness. Morales typically takes the lead from the start, where Biondi is weakest. Morales dives high up into the air, then he knifes down almost vertically into the water; immediately upon entry, he arches up again, shooting forward under the water to emerge ahead of the pack. This style, practiced perhaps most effectively by 1984 gold medalist Steve Lundquist, is widely used, but Morales is better at it than most. He begins his swims quickly, taking an early lead and then hanging on to win. He is not a bad second-half swimmer, but his strength lies in his tremendous speed.

Michael O'Brien

Mike O'Brien must overcome his nagging health problems (see the previous chapter in this book) to be a factor in the

1988 Games. Given that, he could certainly repeat his victory in the fifteen-hundred free, take a medal in the four-hundred, and possibly earn a spot on the American four-by-two-hundred free relay. He could also, as his gold medal in the Pan Ams testifies, do well in the two-hundred backstroke, perhaps finishing in the top three. He has more raw speed than in 1984. He is also older, bigger, stronger, and perhaps wiser, which might help or hurt: He has been there and back, but may lack the hunger of a Morales (who lost his big race in Los Angeles) or of the younger swimmers.

O'Brien's strength is his endurance. Combining his newfound speed with the training he receives under Mark Schubert at Mission Bay, O'Brien could win as many as four medals, two or three of them gold. But first he will have to make the American team, and the competition in his events will be very close.

Dave Wharton

The American men's bright young star is Dave Wharton. In 1986, at the age of seventeen, he broke the American record in the four-hundred-meter individual medley, becoming the youngest male to hold a national record. A year later, at the Pan Pacific Games, he broke the world record in the same event, only to have his mark erased five days later by Hungarian Tamas Darnyi.

Wharton graduated from Germantown Academy, just outside Philadelphia, in 1987, where for five years his coach was Richard Shoulberg, a man known for building great distance swimmers. Wharton has the endurance he will need at the Games, but he is still somewhat untried in major international competition. He spent the World Championships in 1986 violently ill, "drinking Kaopectate by the gallon," in his own words. His 1987 Pan Pacific defeats of then-world record holder Alex Baumann in the two-hundred and four hundred IMs were major steps. He is young enough still to add height and muscle to his frame by the time of the Seoul Games. He will be a sophomore at the University of Southern California, a college teammate of Mike O'Brien.

Because the IM comprises the four strokes swum in succession—butterfly, backstroke, breaststroke, and freestyle—races as they occur are difficult to evaluate unless one knows the competitors. Pablo Morales, who holds the American record in the two-hundred IM, will always lead the field in the early laps, with his strong butterfly. Wharton, on the other hand, is a second-half swimmer, with a noticeably poor backstroke but an outstanding freestyle; he has been world-ranked in distance freestyle events. Over the second half of the IM, few can challenge him. If Wharton is even with the leaders in the four-hundred IM at the halfway point (after the backstroke) he will likely win. But wherever he stands halfway, count on him to close the gap in the finishing laps.

Steven Bentley

Another contender is Steve Bentley, a USC graduate who in 1987 broke Steve Lundquist's two-hundred-meter breaststroke record and became the first American to go under 2:15 in that event. Bentley, who at one time was addicted to cocaine, ranks third in the world, close behind Hungary's Jozsef Szabo and the Soviet Union's Sergei Sokolovskiy. Insiders point to him as a comer.

Also watch: *Melvin Stewart* in the two-hundred fly (one of the most hotly contested races internationally) and *Sean Killion* in the distance freestyles. Both are young and coming up fast.

THE WOMEN'S EVENTS

Remember: The East German women will be strong in every event, especially at the shorter distances, and the D.D.R. should sweep the relay events. In the breaststroke, Silke Horner and Sylvia Gerasch may well finish *several seconds* ahead of any American. Other countries also have their potential winners: Watch the Netherlands' Conny Van Bentum and Romania's Tamara Costache in sprint freestyles, Great Britain's Sarah Hardcastle in the distance freestyles, and Bulgaria's Tania Bogomilova in the breaststroke.

But in certain areas Americans are very strong, and the past two years have shown remarkable improvement in the American women's team, which has suffered a long low spell over the past decade. Several names in particular stand out.

Mary T. Meagher

No swimmer in history has so dominated a stroke, and for so long, as twenty-three-year-old Mary T. Meagher (pronounced "Mah-her") of Louisville, Kentucky. She first set the world record in the two-hundred-meter butterfly in 1979, and she still holds it. Only once over the past eight years has she failed to rank number one in the world in this event. Occasionally—once every two years or so—an East German has come close, and she was beaten in 1982 at the World Championships, but only a near-miracle can stop Meagher at her best in the two-hundred fly.

The one-hundred-meter event is a different story, with Jenna Johnson and a handful of others able to get the start and sprint the full two lengths. Meagher took third in the one-hundred at the World Championships in Madrid in 1986, but she was suffering from a bad case of intestinal flu. She has a rare ability to hold her stroke together through the later stages of the race when other swimmers begin to tire. If Meagher leads "going out" the first half, especially in the two-hundred, it's hard to see anyone else winning. Obviously, too, she is a major asset to the American medley relay team.

Betsy Mitchell

The return of the American women's team (Meagher always being the exception) to the world scene began in 1986, when Betsy Mitchell, a twenty-year-old from the University of Texas: (1) dropped three seconds and broke the world record in the two-hundred backstroke; (2) ranked first in the world in both the one-hundred and the two-hundred back; and (3) grabbed world ranking in the one-hundred and two-hundred freestyles and the two-hundred-meter individual medley. Mitchell became the first American woman since 1981 to break a world record, and regularly finished races three to five seconds ahead of her nearest competitor. Her best time in the two-hundred back is 1.3 seconds ahead of anyone else's.

She stands five feet nine inches tall and weighs a sturdy 150 pounds. A superb softball player from a family of athletes, Mitchell grew up in a small town in eastern Ohio, and is widely known as a tremendous competitor. At her level of the sport, everyone tries to win, but Mitchell stands out, perhaps in the way Steve Lundquist did among the Olympians of 1984. Her college coach, Richard Quick, who will be the U.S. team's coach for the Olympics, says simply, "She's a very fierce competitor." Her prep-school coach, John Trembley of Mercersburg Academy, says that Mitchell has the "killer instinct."

With both speed and endurance, Mitchell is a strong contender for at least the two golds in the backstroke events; she could also be on American relays swimming both backstroke and freestyle. Most important, she is a leader. With broad international experience—gold medals at the Pan Pacific Games, the World Championships, the U.S. Open, and the NCAAs—and consistent world-leading rankings, she is, along with Mary T. Meagher, a valuable team veteran.

Janet Evans

"Little Big Girl," the editors of *Swimming World* called this remarkable young distance swimmer, the third potential star on the women's team, in a January 1987 cover story. Janet Evans is noticeably small, belying popular myths of Amazons in tank suits. In 1985, at the age of thirteen, she first made the finals at Nationals measuring under five feet tall and weighing at most eighty-five pounds. By 1987, at age fifteen, she was five-four and weighed ninety-five pounds. That summer, at the Long Course Nationals, she broke world records in the eight-hundred and the fifteen-hundred freestyle events. She also won the four-hundred free and the four hundred-meter IM. She won the high-point trophy for the meet, scoring 280 points to her nearest competitor's (Amy Shaw) 160, and instantly became the darling of American swimming.

Evans is young enough to look forward to two or even three Olympiads. Her coach at the Fullerton, California, Aquatic Swim Team—FAST, they call themselves—is Bud McAllister, a former Mission Viejo assistant. McAllister says that against tougher competition Evans can go faster than her records and she is getting only stronger with age. "She's a year ahead of schedule," he said in 1987. "She loves to swim and trains more consistently than anyone I've seen."

She'll need that training. When the East Germans had finished their work at the European Championships in late August 1987, only one of Evans's records remained, and that in the fifteen-hundred free. There is no women's fifteen-hundred in the Olympics, only the shorter eight-hundred, where the diminutive Evans may be at a disadvantage. Expect her to go out fast in the four-hundred and eight-hundred freestyle events; she is not generally a "negative splitter" who picks up her pace throughout the race. In the four-hundred-meter IM, her other strong event, she suffers from a relatively poor butterfly and backstroke, and will have to make up ground against the world's best on the breaststroke and especially the freestyle. During the year from 1986 to 1987, she dropped eight seconds in the IM. If she repeats that improvement in 1988, she will break the world record by three seconds.

This girl might do it.

Amy Shaw

Ever since the late sixties, with the notable exception of Tracy Caulkins, the breaststroke has been a weak event for the American women, who typically learn to swim using the crawl (freestyle) and do most of their training in the freestyle as well. Other countries (the Soviet Union, for one) teach their children breaststroke first, and this difference in emphasis continues. It shows up in international competitions.

But in 1987, fifteen-year-old Amy Shaw dropped the American record in the two-hundred-meter breaststroke by nearly one and a half seconds, becoming the first American to swim the event in under two minutes and thirty seconds. She then ranked second in the world.

She is also young, with little international experience but much room to improve. Her coach at Mission Viejo is Terry Stoddard, whose own teenage experiences with coach Mark Schubert are described in the opening chapter of this book. Stoddard has worked with a number of world-class swimmers, and if Shaw continues to improve, she may give the Americans a pleasant surprise.

Dara Torres

In 1987, at the Pan Pacific Games, Dara Torres went 55.86 for the one-hundred free, the first time she had been under 56 and faster than the gold-medal time of the 1984 Olympics. It was her first international victory apart from relays. Her endurance has certainly improved from her teenaged days (she will be twenty-one in 1988), and her training habits and attitude are better than ever; but she still tends to "die" coming back the second half.

She remains almost one and a half seconds behind the world record of East German Kristin Otto, who is still very actively competing. Torres would have to make significant improvements to even hope for a win, and Otto has teammates who will be close to the gold medal. Dara Torres has her work cut out for her.

Also watch: *Jenna Johnson*, with high world rankings in sprint freestyle and butterfly. Six feet tall, 138 pounds: great starts, incredible speed, fades in the longer races. Silver in '84 Olympics one-hundred fly to Meagher; gold on the four-by-one-hundred free relay there. And *Tiffany Cohen*, who won two golds in Los Angeles (four-hundred and eight-hundred free) and nearly broke world records. The question with Cohen is motivation: With gold medals in her pocket, does she care to try again?

The U.S. team has a poor record swimming in countries with unfamiliar cultures: Witness the World Championship catastrophes of Guayaquil, Ecuador, in 1982 and Madrid in 1986. In both cases, intestinal upset decimated the U.S. team. Seoul is an unknown in this regard. The team will train for three weeks before the Games in Australia, which will ease the time-change problem, but it remains to be seen if the U.S. management can overcome the difficulties we often have abroad.

On the other hand, the team itself is probably the strongest the Americans have produced since the late seventies, when Tracy Caulkins, Sippy Woodhead, Brian Goodell, and Jesse Vassallo were at their peaks. The competition in almost every event, male and female, will be strong, and any champions coming out of the swimming events in Seoul will truly deserve to be recognized as such.

Sources and Acknowledgments

HOW I GATHERED THIS INFORMATION MAY BE WORTH SHAR-
ing. Professionally I am a sociologist who studies how
people behave within different kinds of organizations (for
instance, sports teams). As a teenager in the late 1960s
I enthusiastically competed as a member of several
swimming teams, although never beyond the statewide
level. During college and after, my interest in the sport
waned, and only in the past few years have I resumed
some coaching, largely volunteer, with an age-group swim
team. In January 1983, looking for a new research topic, I
decided to do something involving swimming—and with
the 1984 Olympics coming up, the opportunity was perfect
to look at world-class performances. Mission Viejo was the
obvious choice of venues if one wanted to see top-rank
swimming.

So I called the Mission Viejo Recreation Center, which
houses the pools and the team, and asked the secretary,

Martha Lee Pyykko, if I could come out to California and watch a few practices. To shorten a long story, I did that, coming to early-morning practices and sitting in the rain, minding my own business, watching closely for four days. Two months later I returned and sat there again—rarely talking with anyone, hardly moving, so afraid was I of being thrown out (rules forbid any spectators during practices; I think the rules were waived because I had flown all the way from New York just to watch). After that second week-long visit, Mark Schubert, the Nadadores' head coach—with whom I had exchanged perhaps thirty words in a week's time—told me I could visit anytime, go anywhere with the team, and talk with anyone on it. He seemed impressed by my patience.

I began flying to Mission Viejo at every opportunity, observing at training sessions, listening at team meetings, talking with the swimmers, watching them in meets. I traveled to the U.S. International meet in Texas in January 1984, the U.S. Spring Nationals, the Olympic Trials in June, the Olympic team training camp, and the Olympic Games. Throughout I was living with the Mission Viejo team—taking the same airplanes, eating all my meals with them, sharing their hotel quarters, riding to and from the pool with them. In the summer of 1984 I lived with several of the Mission Viejo coaches in Orange County and, over take-out Chinese food, learned more about swimming than this book can pass on. During the same summer I attended workouts at the Olympic Training Camp, which was held in Mission Viejo, and interviewed swimmers at the Holiday Inn-Laguna Hills, where they lived during the camp. I was allowed into the Olympic team's closed practices, mainly because I minded my own business. I read innumerable books on swimming, mostly bad, and twenty years' worth of *Sports Illustrated* articles on swimming, mostly good. Over the past fifteen years I have read more issues of *Swimming World* magazine than I care to count.

But the main source for the research was just watching swimmers for many hours, taking photographs, doing interviews—having conversations with veteran coaches and hot young coaches, with Olympic swimmers from 1976 and age-groupers fresh out of North Carolina and Chicago, with swimsuit marketers and sportswriters and parents.

As a result I learned a good deal about swimming—the physiology of training, the physics of stroke technique, the psychology of coaching, the organization of teams, the history of the sport. Yet I am not professionally affiliated with top-rank swimming. My income doesn't depend on pleasing a parents' group or saying nice things about other coaches or working well with certain officials. I don't rely on the swimming world for either my career advancement or my personal gratifications. I do have a few friends in top-rank swimming, but mostly they are people unlikely to be offended by the cynical comments of a college professor. Officials of U.S. Swimming seem to believe that this book will advertise swimming or provide them with development strategies; they will probably be disappointed.

My independence from swimming, I hope, makes this book at least somewhat different. Most writing on swimming to this point has been clearly ideological: *Swimming World* magazine is a house organ for the dominant factions in the sport (some coaches refer to it jokingly as "California Swimming . . . and Friends"), and the staff, dependent on the athletes and coaches they cover for subscriptions, are thus unable to tell much of what goes on—about the vicious anti-Semitism suffered by Mark Spitz from the swimming community throughout his career, to pick one example. Books about swimming are usually technical manuals read only by coaches, or disguised as exercise books; occasionally there is a post-Olympic memoir glorifying the latest gold medalist ("It took a lot of pain and hard work, but it was all worth it"). With two notable exceptions—Dawn Fraser's *Below the Surface* and Don

Schollander's *Deep Water*—none of these books analyzes how the sport is organized, who runs it, or why certain teams are better than others, with any real detachment or intellectual rigor. These two books were written by superb athletes with sharp minds who, for different reasons, had achieved an independence from swimming and so were able to tell some unpleasant truths (note the similar implications of their titles). With a similar independence, *Sports Illustrated,* attracting readers far beyond the swimming community, can point out the embarrassments as well as the achievements of the sport. There are weaknesses in *SI*'s coverage, but excessive partisanship is not one of them.

So to those readers who are looking for a glamorous story of heroes in victory, or for a lurid exposé ("Chambliss rips away the veil of hypocrisy, lays bare the seamy underside of big-time swimming") in these pages—I can only offer a mild apology. If there are any heroes or villains in this story (and the reader alone can judge that) they are approachable ones, people with whom you can sit down and eat a plate of spaghetti—or, more in line with their caloric needs, three plates of spaghetti and a full loaf of garlic bread.

The research reported here was made possible by the cooperation of Mark Schubert, the staff, and the swimmers of the Mission Viejo Nadadores. Without Schubert's support this book could not have been written.

Terry Stoddard answered many questions and provided daily help in ways too numerous to mention, and he offered support before anyone else cared.

Larry Liebowitz, the Junior Nationals team coach at Mission Viejo during the time of this book (and probably one of the finest unsung coaches in America), taught me the most and gave me a home in Mission to boot. I continue to learn from him.

Hamilton College provided substantial financial support, both in faculty research aid and in granting a year's leave, backed by a Margaret Bundy Scott faculty fellowship. I am especially grateful to former Dean C. Duncan Rice for his active support in the early stages of the project.

Several colleagues in sociology helped with the research and writing at various stages. Randall Collins, David Gray, David Stevenson, and Eviatar Zerubavel were all encouraging, and in various ways they helped bring the project back to its crucial themes when I began to get lost telling stories. Kai Erikson continues to be an invaluable mentor, model, and friend. Daniel J. Ryan, Jr., performed a masterful job of editing the final manuscript before it went to the publisher, rewriting innumerable tortured sentences and suggesting countless new ways of making some difficult points. I am especially grateful to him.

The manuscript benefited from the detailed readings of Alex Chambliss, a professional editor motivated by personal concern. At one crucial stage of the project David Halberstam gave valuable advice, which I took. Regina Kecht's patient listening to and detailed comments on an early draft, as well as unfailing friendship in times of need, have both been appreciated more than she can know. Doug Stumpf of William Morrow and Company improved the narrative significantly, and has been the editor I hoped for.

As this is my first book, I want to thank my father and mother and Penny Rosel, for contributions beyond explanation.

Some of the information in this book comes from articles by John Weyler and Tracy Dodds of the *Los Angeles Times* and by Craig Neff of *Sports Illustrated*. I am happy to acknowledge here the use of this material and to thank those writers for doing a good job of covering a sport that most reporters don't take very seriously. In addition, much material was used from the Swimming Hall of Fame Library in Fort Lauderdale, Florida, and from various anonymous librarians with whom I dealt over the phone; they will receive a complimentary copy of this book and my thanks.

Research assistants in the projects worked on manuscript revisions, took and developed and printed photographs, made travel and housing arrangements, compiled statistics, secured press passes, handled correspondence, did literature searches, photocopied rough drafts, criticized bad ideas, typed up rough drafts, alphabetized lists of names, and harassed me until I finally put words down on paper. In Los Angeles they conducted several of the interviews. I am grateful for their help. In Los Angeles: Polly Adema and Gary Morris. In Clinton, New York: Meg Burch, Julie Dansingburg, Susan Plunkett, Julie Reinshagen, and especially Jody Speier. For two summers Brad Albert was more a collaborator than an assistant, and he virtually co-wrote sections of the book. He probably knows this book better than anyone save its author who is, of course, responsible for any errors of fact or interpretation.

Below are listed the swimmers, coaches, and officials whose words and thoughts appear in this book. Almost all of the interviews with them were conducted face to face (not by telephone), and many of those conversations lasted several hours, sometimes repeated at intervals over a two-year period. Thanks to the following: Paul Asmuth, David Barnes, Bill Barrett, Martha Bass, Bill Bell, Keith Bell, Don Berger, Paul Bergen, Steve Berizzi, Bernie Boglioli, Wendy Boglioli, Scott Brackett, Dave Burgering, Mike Burton, Rick Carey, Amy Caulkins, Chris Cavanaugh, Sherm Chavoor, Jeanne Childs, Mark Clarke, Tiffany Cohen, John Collins, Tony Corbisiero, Jim Cornish, James Counsilman, Dave Cowell, Craig Crozier, Sean Dailey, Peter Daland, Jeff Dimond, Ray Essick, Tom Fay, Ellen Feldman, Geoff Gaberino, Rowdy Gaines, Don Gambril, Haik Gharibians, Don Graham, Don Greene, Steve Gregg, David Guthrie, George Haines, Dick Hannula, Keith Hanssen, Andy

Hathaway, Brad Hering, Channon Hermstad, Don Hickmann, Todd Hickmann, Charlie Hodgson, Nancy Hogshead, Jennifer Hooker, Richey Hughey, Mitch Ivey, Dan Jorgensen, Frank Keefe, Patrick Kennedy, Chris Kirchner, Terry Laughlin, Laurie Lehner, Larry Liebowitz, Dave Louden, Steve Lundquist, Bud McAllister, Scott MacFarland, Ann McPherson, John Mason, Mary T. Meagher, Kay Meyer, Michael Meyer, Craig Neff, Sandy Neilson, Jennifer Nye, Connie O'Brien, Mike O'Brien, Ron O'Brien, Phyllis Orcutt, Shannon Orcutt, Mary Joan Pennington, Kevin Perry, Ricardo Prado, Dennis Pursley, Martha Lee Pyykko, Ris Pyykko, Richard Quick, Eddie Reese, Randy Reese, Rich Saeger, Nancy Schleuter (the mother), Nancy Schleuter (the daughter), Bill Schmidt, Mark Schubert, Charles Silvia, An Simmons, Dick Sloan, Chris Smith, Terry Stoddard, Andy Strenk, Shirley Sturgeon, Radine Thomas, Dave Thompson, Dara Torres, Doug Towne, Ken Treadway, Melissa Trueblood, Diane Ursin, Jesse Vassallo, Mary Wayte, Karin Werth, Gil Westwell, John Weyler, Amy White, Julie Williams, and Ron Young.

And finally, Laurie Moses and Theresa George made daily contributions too many to mention, for which I am grateful.

Sources and Acknowledgments